## *in the*
## PEAK DISTRICT

*John Morrison*

*25 scenic circular walks including traditional country inns*

**Dalesman**

First published in 1997 by Dalesman
*an imprint of*
Country Publications Ltd
The Water Mill, Broughton Hall,
Skipton
North Yorkshire BD23 3AG
www.countrypublications.co.uk


Revised edition 2009

Text © John Morrison 1997, 2009
Illustrations © Donald Dakeyne 1997, except p15 by Christine
Isherwood 2009
Maps by Jeremy Ashcroft, except p14 by Gelder Design & Mapping


Cover: Bull's Head, Monyash, by Geoff Cowton


ISBN 978-1-85568-127-9

Printed by Amadeus Press, Cleckheaton

# Pub Walks

*in the*

# PEAK DISTRICT

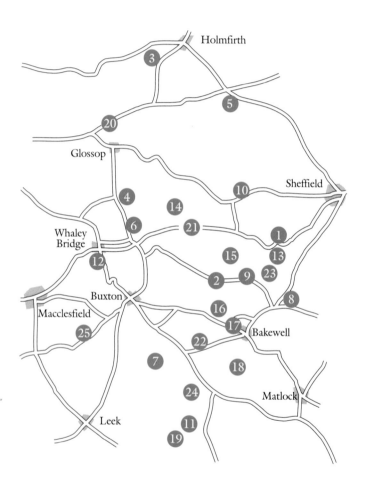

# $\mathcal{W}$ALKS

# INTRODUCTION

Here is a collection of splendid walks which cover the length and breadth of the Peak National Park. They cover a wide range of landscapes too, from intimate riverside rambles to the open moortops and gritstone edges where you can lengthen your stride. All the walks can be attempted confidently by walkers who are reasonably fit. Weather conditions are notoriously fickle, however, so be sure to pack wet-weather gear along with the sandwiches.

The route descriptions and maps should provide trouble-free way-finding. However, it is advisable to carry the appropriate Ordnance Survey map too. This will add to the interest of the walks, by giving details of other landscape features you'll see along the way. More importantly, in the unlikely event of losing your way, an OS map will help to get you back on track. Don't consider tackling some of the wilder country without a map.

It's a sign of the times that so many pubs are becoming walker-friendly. You'll get a warm welcome at all the pubs featured in this book, especially if you leave muddy boots outside. What could be better: an interesting walk followed by a good pint and an appetising meal? Walks number 1, 2, 8, 11, 12, 13, 19, 21 and 25 have alternative starting points, marked on the maps (and with * in the text) for those who prefer to walk *to* – rather than *from* – a pub.

*This book is dedicated to Sheila Bowker,*
*walker and cricketer.*

# FOX HOUSE INN

NEAR HATHERSAGE

*Despite its proximity to Sheffield, this walk explores a wild gritstone landscape*

DISTANCE: 4 miles (7km)
ALLOW: 2 hours
MAP: OS Landranger 110
TERRAIN: Easy
PARKING: Free car-park adjacent to the pub's own car-park

Fox House Inn lies on the main A625 road between Hathersage and the suburbs of Sheffield. Considering how close it is to Sheffield, on the eastern edge of the national park, Fox House Inn enjoys splendidly rural surroundings. In the immediate vicinity are some of the region's finest gritstone landscapes – Stanage Edge being particularly popular with climbers.

The pub was built in the late 18th century, as a shepherd's cottage, and is thought to have been the model for Whitecross, in Charlotte Brontë's novel Jane Eyre. There are two large lounges, open fires and an extensive menu, supplemented by daily specials. Food is available from 12-3pm and evening meals (at weekends, all day from 12-9pm). Tel: 01433-630374.

Walk down the A625 from Fox House Inn, signed to Castleton and Hathersage. After 500m bear right, on a broad track, through two gates and into open country: rocks, heather

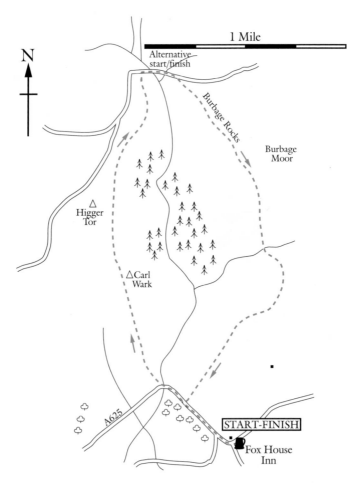

and bracken. Follow the track as it heads toward the rocky outcrop of Carl Wark. When the track bears right, after a pair of stone gateposts, your route is left, on a lesser path, still aiming towards the outcrop. Cross

Burbage Brook in a single leap and scramble to the top of Carl Wark.

*There was a prehistoric hill-fort sited on this flat, grassy plateau, and part of a wall still stands. Opinions about its age are divided, however, and it may have been built since the Roman occupation.*

There are splendid views from this vantage, including Mam Tor and the Great Ridge, with plenty more to come as you link up with a path at the far end of Carl Wark and head downhill towards the larger rocky outcrop of Higger Tor. Climb up the right-hand side of the tor, quite steeply near the top. At the far side of the outcrop you approach a fork of tracks; take the right-hand option to walk parallel to a road ahead.

The walking is easy until you scramble up a few rocks to

reach the road by the left of two stone bridges. (*) Walk to the right, along the road, for just 200m. Take either of two stiles on the right to join a path that climbs to the top of Burbage Rocks, another gritstone edge that's popular with climbers. For the next mile (1.5km) the path stays close to the edge.

When the path forks, keep left, uphill, soon crossing another path by two small cairns. Continue uphill, to the top of another gritstone edge; follow a path along the top until, at the end of the rocks, the path makes a gradual descent towards Fox House Inn. Cross a pair of stiles to reach the A625, and walk left, up the road and back to the pub.

# THREE STAGS' HEADS

W A R D L O W   M I R E S

*A wide variety of landscapes from dramatic limestone cliffs to intimate woodland with a choice of several pubs on the way*

DISTANCE:
7 miles (11km)
ALLOW:
3 hours
MAP:
OS Outdoor Leisure 24
TERRAIN:
Easy
PARKING:
Pay & display car park to the rear of the Monsal Head Hotel (and some free parking spaces nearby, on the road to Little Longstone)

Wardlow Mires, near the junction of the A623 and B6465, is a tiny hamlet which was once part of the Chatsworth Estate. The Three Stags' Heads Inn is housed in a seventeenth-century farmhouse, and the interior has changed little over the years, with its stone-flagged floors and open fire. There is a choice of real ales (just don't ask for lager) and an imaginative selection of home-cooked meals using local produce, available 12.30pm-4pm and 7.30pm-9.30pm. Tel 01298 872268.

Take the road opposite the Monsal Head Hotel and walk into the village of Little Longstone. Pass a pinfold (where stray livestock used to be corralled) and the Packhorse pub. The last house on the road is Orchard Cottage; immediately afterwards there are three entrances — to a field, a walled path and a house set back from the road. Take the middle option, through a metal gate onto the walled track, to a stile.

Bear right to follow a field-path beside a wall, behind the house. Cross two more stiles to reach Dale

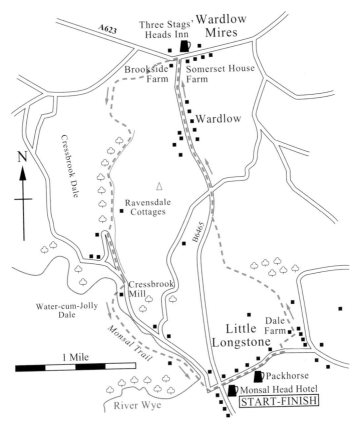

Farm. Join a firm track to the left, uphill, through a pastoral landscape of fields. The track narrows to a path after a field entrance, with flowery verges and hedges to either side.

Look out for a metal gate on the right, close to a stile and a sign indicating a picnic area. Go right here and immediately across another stile to join a good grassy track uphill. The track soon narrows between a fence and a wall as you take a step-stile in a wall. Cross a field in the direction of a conical hill in the middle distance. Keep right after a stone water trough to cross four more fields via stiles. The last stile brings you to a road.

Go right, along the road, and through the village of Wardlow. Walk down to the main A623 road where you'll find the Three Stags' Heads Inn and, hopefully, a seat by the fire.

Retrace a few steps; immediately beyond the turn-off to Wardlow is Brookside Farm. Walk directly in front of the farmhouse and through a gate which gives access to a grassy walled track.

*As indicated by an information panel, you are now entering the valley of Cressbrook Dale, a national nature reserve and, in summer, a profusion of wildflowers.*

Walk downhill, passing limestone scars and outcrops. Ignore a path, left, to Peter's Stone, a curiously shaped limestone outcrop, and keep to the bottom of this delectable, steep-sided valley. Walk through scrubby woodland, and cross a wooden footbridge over a beck (often dry in summer). The path continues through meadows and delightful woodland, emerging onto a metalled track by the attractive grouping of Ravensdale Cottages.

*High up, on the left, looms Ravencliffe Crags, popular with climbers.*

Follow the track ahead, uphill, to meet a road. Go left here, now downhill. Where another road joins from the right, you will find a large millpond on your left.

*On the right is Cressbrook Mill. It is an ambitious example of industrial architecture, dating back to 1815, and its Palladian-styled gables make it look, at first glance, as if it might be an industrialist's home rather than his workplace. The bell in the cupola was used to summon the workers, many of whom — including children — were housed in nearby Apprentices Row. The mill replaced an earlier mill on the same site, built in 1783 by Richard Arkwright, who, by exploiting water power, did so much to mechanise the textile industries.*

At the mill entrance (near the road junction) take a foot-path signed 'Monsal Trail'. A path takes you to the right of the mill, passing a tea shop created out of a bizarre, castellated, mock-Gothic folly, and around a builders' yard. Turn immediately left to take a footbridge over the River Wye, where the water cascades over a weir.

*The river was dammed to create a large millpond that now fills the valley, which goes by the intriguing name of Water-cum-Jolly Dale. Man-made though it may be, this is a peaceful spot, with the water hemmed in by trees and steep limestone cliffs.*

Beyond the bridge, follow a path to the right, uphill. At the top of a bank, bear left to follow another Monsal Trail sign. Join a stony track that takes a level course through the broad, wooded valley of Upperdale. Ahead, on the horizon, is your next objective, the Monsal Head Hotel. But first you must take a gate to join the trackbed of what was once the Midland Railway line, which is now being promoted as the Monsal Trail footpath. Pass the scant remains of Monsal Dale station.

*The line used to carry walkers into the heart of the Peak as well as goods such as limestone quarried in the valley.*

Walk through a cutting and beneath a bridge, to cross the tall viaduct over the River Wye that you will also encounter in the Monsal Head Hotel walk. When you reach the blocked-up tunnel entrance, bear left on a path uphill, through more dense woodland.

Keep right at a fingerpost and climb steeply up to Monsal Head, to enjoy the view down the valley you have just walked: one of the loveliest views in the national park.

# FLEECE INN

HOLME

*A bracing walk exploring the little corner of the Peak National Park that lies in West Yorkshire*

DISTANCE: 5 miles (9km)
ALLOW: 2 hours
MAP: OS Landranger 110
TERRAIN: Moderate; some open moorland
PARKING: Limited car parking in Holme village

Yorkshire folk will be reassured to learn that this walk explores the northeast corner of the Peak National Park without ever leaving God's Own County. The Holme Valley, stretching south from Huddersfield, is punctuated by characterful little villages, traditionally reliant on the textile industries, including Holmfirth, now more widely known as the 'Last of the Summer Wine' town.

*To those approaching the national park via the Holme Valley, the village of Holme is almost the last outpost of civilisation on the A6024. Beyond Holme the 12-mile drive to Glossop takes motorists through some of the wildest country in the north. No wonder this road, along with the Snake Pass a few miles to the south, is one of the first to get snowed up each winter.*

The Fleece Inn is a cosy pub that offers a warm welcome to those walkers considerate enough to remove their muddy boots. There is even a hitching rail and trough round the back for those who arrive on horseback; appropriate since the Fleece was once a livery stable catering for trains of laden packhorse ponies.

Photographs on the wall recall the terrible flood of Whit Monday, 1944, when the Holme Valley – and, in particular, the little town of Holmfirth – was devastated by floodwater. Food is available Tuesday to Saturday from 12-2pm, and 7-9pm, and throughout the day on summer Sundays. Tel: 01484-683449.

Walk left from the pub along the road for just 50m, and bear left up a road (the first few metres are cobbled). Walk 150m up the road and take a gate on the right, opposite a house called The Nook. The gate gives access to a walled track, signed as part of the Kirklees Way. Follow this track to get long views up the Holme Valley, with Emley Moor TV mast looking like an exclamation mark at the end.

A field-path, punctuated by gap-stiles in walls, gradually leads you towards a reservoir. Just 75m from the water's edge, bear left along a more substantial path. Cross a tiny beck on a wooden bridge, take a kissing gate, then follow the path through a gate in a wall. Walk downhill, via steep steps, to take a causeway between two expanses of water: Bilberry Reservoir to the left, Digley Reservoir to the right.

*In 1852 the dam of Bilberry Reservoir burst, transforming the normally placid River Holme into a raging torrent. Far worse than the later flood of 1944, this tragedy claimed 81 lives.*

At the far side of the reservoir follow the path left, uphill, bearing sharp right after a metal gate. Beyond a blue Yorkshire Water sign you bear left along a broader track between dry-stone walls. Follow the track, on a gradual uphill gradient, as it goes sharp right, then sharp left at a T-junction of tracks, soon passing a pair of barns.

After the path wiggles a bit more, you have more excellent views behind you across Digley Reservoir and up the Holme Valley. Pass another pair of barns, then a farmhouse that enjoys the same valley view. 100m beyond the farmhouse take a step-stile in the wall on your left, to join a field-path accompanying a wall down into Marsden Clough.

Take a stile and walk downhill, to cross the beck on a wooden footbridge (if you need a sandwich break, this is the place). The path ahead is clear, bearing left, uphill, onto open, unenclosed moorland: the haunt of curlews, lapwings and red grouse. Your path soon levels out and

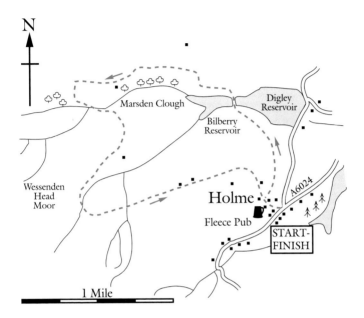

N

Marsden Clough

Digley Reservoir

Bilberry Reservoir

Wessenden Head Moor

Holme

Fleece Pub

A6024

START-FINISH

1 Mile

bears right, around Hey Clough. A long left curve then takes you downhill, crossing little becks, until the path climbs the opposite flank of Hey Clough.

Your path levels out, and joins a more substantial grassy track, as open moorland gives way to fields once again. The track, now between walls, is ruler-straight, with Emley Moor mast a prominent feature on the far horizon. Tracks join – first from the right, then from the left – but your way is ahead, along the cinder track. After a solitary house the track becomes metalled; follow this road downhill and back into Holme village.

# THE SPORTSMAN

*A breezy exploration of the lower Kinder fells, with tempting views up the the Kinder plateau*

DISTANCE: 5 miles (9km)
ALLOW: 2½ hours
MAP: OS Outdoor Leisure 1
TERRAIN: Easy
PARKING: On the road adjacent to the Sportsman pub or, 300m further up Kinder Road, in Bowden Bridge pay and display car-park

Hayfield, a pleasant little village now happily by-passed by the A624 road and lying halfway between Glossop and Chapel-en-le-Frith, has a unique place in walking history. It was from here, in April 1932, that a troupe of about 500 ramblers, frustrated at being barred from the Kinder moors by obstructive landowners, embarked on a mass trespass. The protest, though peaceful, culminated with the ringleaders being jailed; the resulting furore hastened the opening up of more of our uplands to ramblers.

Being merely a cul-de-sac that ends at Kinder Reservoir, Kinder Road isn't the easiest of thoroughfares to find. You can reach it via Bank Street (near the bridge over the River Sett, in the middle of Hayfield) or the road that branches off by the Pack Horse pub. Once these roads combine, the Sportsman is about 1km further on.

The Sportsman offers a warm welcome and cosy bars; it is cool on hot summer days and – thanks to log fires – reassuringly warm on the coldest of winter days. Food from

the extensive menu is served from 12-2pm (every day except Monday) and 7-9pm (every day except Sunday). Tel: 01663-741565.

Walk left out of the pub (or Bowden Bridge car park) and walk along Kinder Road, with woodland to the left, and fields and the River Kinder to the right. Just past a pebble-dashed bungalow are the gates and access road for Kinder Reservoir. Bear to the right in front of them, cross the river and take the metalled track uphill (a sign indicates this is a Public Bridleway to Farlands). Beyond

Farlands – a house and a farm – the huge grassy dam of Kinder Reservoir comes into view.

Look out, at a point where the track briefly broadens, for a gate on the right, signed as a Bridleway to Stoney Ford. Go right here, on a field-path uphill, to follow the edge of a conifer plantation. Immediately after another gate, bear right, uphill, with terrific views opening up on the left to Kinder Reservoir and up to the bleak heights of the Kinder plateau.

Your path follows a tumble-down wall for 100m, levels off and brings you to a gate in a fence. Continue along a field-path, heading for the right-hand end of the Kinder plateau ahead, pass a wall-corner then a stile. At a signpost marking the boundary of open country, join a walled path to the right – soon continuing straight ahead to follow the right-hand wall.

Turn sharp right at a wall-end to another gate and stile. You have more great views from here, towards the Edale and Sett Valleys. After the stile you have a choice of track; keep left on a well-defined path across Harry Moor in the general direction of South Head, a distinctive conical hill on the horizon. You have level walking until the path descends and offers another choice of route. Take the right-hand fork to arrive shortly at a pair of gates.

The track on the far side is an old packhorse road; follow it to the right, downhill, to a gate. A four-way sign offers the track ahead as the way back to Hayfield. Continue down the stony track, between a wall and a fence, to reach another track at a hairpin bend. Keep right here, crossing a beck, to a glade of trees and Coldwell Clough

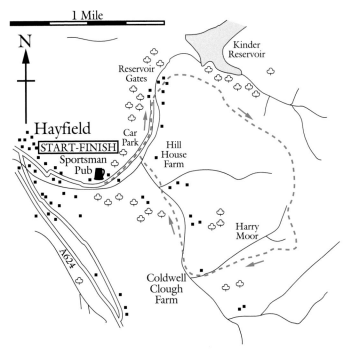

Farm. Follow the track – now metalled – downhill, to another fork of tracks, and two gates.

Take the left-hand gate, cross a little stone bridge, and follow a sandy track uphill. Ignore turnoffs and keep to the track – soon downhill – through gates, onto a minor road. Cross the river and keep left along the road to come out on Kinder Road at Bowden Bridge, by the confluence of the rivers Sett and Kinder. The car-park is ahead of you (turn left, along the road, to return to the Sportsman pub).

# WAGGON AND HORSES

## LANGSETT

*Water, woods and open moor on a concessionary path courtesy of Yorkshire Water*

DISTANCE:
3¹/₂ miles
(6km)
ALLOW: 2
hours
MAP:
Ordnance
Survey
Landranger
110
TERRAIN:
Easy
PARKING:
Public car-park
just 200 metres
north of the
Waggon and
Horses, on the
same side of
the A616

The little hamlet of Langsett lies on the eastern boundary of the national park, on the A616 between Huddersfield and Sheffield. Or, rather, it is just off the A616, and most drivers will speed by unawares. Those who do stop at the national park's car-park will find that Langsett Barn, a splendid building dating back to 1621 – as indicated by a datestone – has been given a new lease of life as a tourist information centre. The interior, with its 'post and truss' construction, is worth viewing in its own right.

The Waggon and Horses pub offers a panoramic view across the water of Langsett Reservoir, especially for those enjoying a drink at one of the many tables laid out on the lawn. Good home-made fare is available from 12-2pm, and 7-9pm. To get from the car-park to the pub, walk around Langsett Barn, and take a track to the right, past two groups of houses. Tel: 01226-763147.

Leave the car-park by a gate at the end furthest from the road, to follow a path downhill into conifer woodland. Keep left at a fork, through tree cover so dense that the woodland floor is bare. Keep to this path, about 50m from the edge of Langsett Reservoir.

*The reservoir is one of three reservoirs created here, in the Upper Don Valley, by Sheffield Corporation, to assuage the thirst of South Yorkshire towns and expanding industries.*

Soon you follow the path left, and closer to the water, to detour round a fenced-off area of woodland. The walking is easy, through a mixed woodland of conifers and broad-leaved trees, as the reservoir narrows. Continue, a little uphill, on a fenced path through a plantation of young trees, to join another path leading straight downhill to Brook House Bridge, crossing the River Don as it drains into the reservoir. The grassy river banks on the right make a popular picnic site.

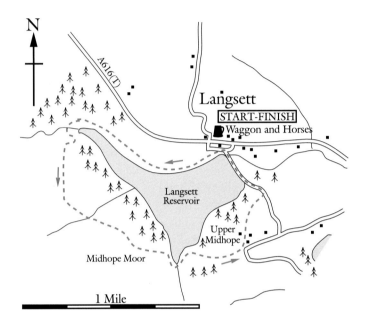

Across the bridge keep left on a path that soon climbs quite steeply to skirt more conifer woodland. Emerge onto open heather moorland and keep climbing. Soon your efforts are rewarded by fine views back over the reservoir, the Upper Don Valley and one of the modern windfarms that seem to inspire so much heated debate in Pennine communities.

Towards the top of the hill you come across a post which bears one of Yorkshire Water's blue waymarking arrows. Bear left here on a path that goes gradually downhill, past a ruined building, through a gate, to follow what is by now a broader cinder track.

Walk downhill to skirt a conifer wood on your left, and
follow the track down to a bridge over another little
river. The path bears left, through a metal gate, and then
right – away from the reservoir and back into mixed
woodland. At the end of the wood take a gate that leads
you onto a metalled waterworks road. After a traffic
barrier you come to a public road at a sharp bend. Go
left, just before a road-sign indicating Upper Midhope
and Langsett, up a grassy walled path. Walk between a
house and a barn, then walk immediately left for just
25m, to follow the Public Bridleway sign to your right
and take a metalled track through pasture. Skirt a small
wood and emerge onto a minor road.

Go left to cross the dam of Langsett Reservoir and
continue along the road until you reach the busy A616
and the Waggon and Horses pub. To return to the car-
park, walk around the pub and take a track past houses
and Langsett Barn.

# THE LAMB INN

*Gorgeous views from a grassy ridge at the western edge of the national park*

**DISTANCE:** 4¹/₂ miles (8km)
**ALLOW:** 2 hours
**MAP:** OS Landranger 110
**TERRAIN:** Easy
**PARKING:** At the Lamb Inn, on the A624 midway between Hayfield and Chapel-en-le-Frith

The upgrading of the A624 into a busy trunk road has screened the Lamb Inn from passing traffic. Customers can now sit in the beer garden out front, enjoying a drink and a meal in what is now a more tranquil cul-de-sac. Pub walkers are welcome to park in the large car-park. The inscription over the pub entrance reveals a date of 1769, and the interior retains a homely feel. Food from an extensive menu is served from 12-2.30pm and 6-9.30pm; food is available all day at weekends. Tel 01663-750519.

Walk out of the pub to the main road. Walk left for just 75m, cross the road and take the 'Private Road' to Monk's Meadows. Walk down the track (it is a right of way for walkers). At the second cattle grid, just before you reach the farm, take a metal gate on the right to join a waymarked footpath between a wall and a fence.

After 100m take a stile in the fence on the left and follow the path downhill along the field-edge. Take a stile at the bottom right-hand corner of the field, and another stile 20m further, to continue on a path that skirts woodland and passes another house. The path, now squeezed between a fence and a wall, soon emerges at a minor road opposite the elaborate gateposts of Ashen Clough.

Go right, uphill, to arrive at a house with the intriguing name of Peep O'Day. The name is explained if you look at the inscription over the front door – James and Mary Goddard 1841 – featuring a small window, shaped like an eye, which catches the first rays of the sun each morning.

Your path turns off to the left, just before you reach the house. Cross a stile onto a stony track. Immediately there is a choice of route, as detailed on a sign erected by the Peak and Northern Footpaths Society. Keep to the track, uphill, signed to Birch Vale via Grouse Inn. You begin a long climb that offers increasingly wide views: towards Hayfield on the right, and Chinley on the left.

Continue uphill, past a gate and new barn. Ignore a track leading off right at the top of the hill; keep left, now slightly downhill on the stony track. Through a gate at the bottom, follow the track up to Hills Farm. Then keep left, through a gate, to take a well-defined, grassy track uphill towards another farm, Whiterakes. Pass the back of the farm and keep climbing the flank of the hill, enjoying tremendous views all the while.

*Soon you come across the first sign of the quarrying activity that once made this ridge – Cracken Edge – ring loud with noise and industry. Slate from these quarries was used to roof many of the buildings in the vicinity. Soon there are more substantial quarrying remains, including extensive screes of stones extending down the hill.*

The path levels out as you pass, down on your left, the remains of the winding engine that provided the best method of transporting slate from the Cracken Edge quarries down into the valley. Beyond the winding gear

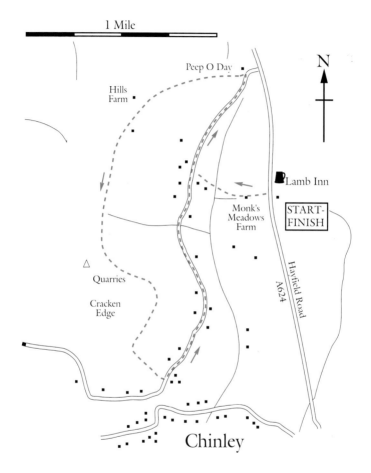

you come to a fork of tracks; keep left towards a walled track. Walk down the hollow-way (or the path that runs beside it) and join the walled track. It soon bears right, offering views across to Chapel-en-le-Frith, and becomes another hollow-way.

About 75m past where another track joins from the right, look for a stile on the left and take an indistinct path steeply downhill. Cross more stiles before the path runs between houses and down to a minor road. Walk left along the road, slightly uphill, past houses, soon having fields on both sides once again. You have about a mile of road-walking before you come to more houses on the right and the gates of Ashen Clough on the left.

From here you locate a footpath sign on the right and retrace the steps you took at the beginning of the walk. That is: take a narrow enclosed path, then a field-path uphill to skirt Monk's Meadows Farm. Follow the farm track up to the road and back to the Lamb Inn.

# HORSESHOE INN

LONGNOR

*An exploration of pleasant pastoral countryside and the infant River Manifold*

DISTANCE: 6½ miles (11 km)
ALLOW: 3 hours
MAP: OS Outdoor Leisure 24
TERRAIN: Easy (best in summer when some boggy bits are drier underfoot)
PARKING: Free parking in the old market place

The Horseshoe Inn, a handsome building overlooking Longnor's cobbled market place, offers a warm welcome to walkers. Half of the cosy bar has a flagged floor, so walking boots aren't a problem. No need to hurry your walk to ensure you get some lunch: food is served from 12-9.30pm. Tel: 01298-83262.

*Longnor's Victorian market-hall and market place, surrounded by more pubs than you'd imagine a village of this size might logically require, are reminders that Longnor was, a century ago, a market town of some importance. But economic decline in the local farming community, and the unfulfilled promise that the railway would come, undermined the village's prosperity.*

From the crossroads in the centre of the village, take a road signed to Royal Cottage and Leek. When the road swings left, downhill, take a track ahead. Beyond the Vicarage the track becomes rougher as it descends towards Gauledge Farm.

Immediately before the farmhouse take a gap stile on the left, to take a field-path around the farm. Follow a wall via two more gap-stiles, then head downhill – bearing slightly left – to pick up another gap-stile and a slab-bridge across a beck.

Continue straight ahead, uphill, towards a wall-end. Take a step-stile over the wall and go straight on, keeping the wall to your left, to Fawside Farm. Walk through the farmyard, then bear slightly left (follow a fingerpost) to a stile in a fence. Follow a wall until it bears right; bear left here (avoiding boggy areas) to reach an unassuming little bridge over a beck that will soon unite with others to form the River Manifold. Keep straight ahead, to cross another beck on a wooden footbridge, then uphill to a gate that gives onto a road.

Walk left along the road, uphill; at the top of the hill go right along a road signed Fawfieldhead and Newton. Go almost immediately right again along a road marked as a cul-de-sac. The walking is easy, with woodland on the left and pleasant valley views towards Hollinsclough opening up on the right: a pastoral landscape of scattered farms, copses and field-walls. Pass the entrance to Longnor Wood Caravan Park; when the track bears right, over a cattle grid to Hill End Farm, you should keep ahead, downhill, via a grassy hollow-way. Through a metal gate and past farm buildings, you join a farm-track downhill.

When it bears right, take a stile on the left and follow a footpath arrow across a field; more stiles help to guide you around Slack Farm and to join a farm-track that soon reaches a road. Go left here, but after just 100m, as the road bears left, take a stile on the right, by a field gate.

Follow the wall downhill to a stile; immediately afterwards take another stile on the left to descend to a tiny beck. Hop over and walk uphill, then go left to accompany a substantial hedgerow, soon descending to a stile in a fence.

Keep straight ahead across pasture to a stile and wooden footbridge (if it's still damaged, cross where the tractors cross, a few metres away). Walk straight across a field, uphill; at the top take a stile on the right, by a metal gate. Keep to the left of a barn to take another stile, then follow a hedgerow ahead, slightly downhill, to a stile at

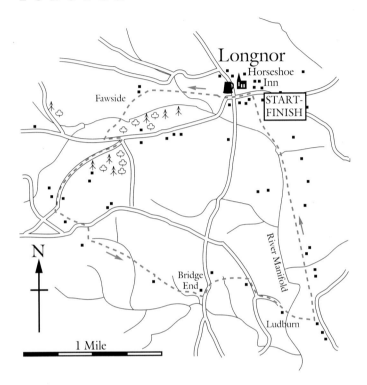

the bottom of the field. Keep following the hedgerow, then cross a tiny beck on a wooden footbridge. Meet a road immediately to the right of a house, and close to a stone bridge spanning Blake Brook.

Walk left along the road, uphill. At a left-hand bend, go right (between chevron signs) to immediately take a gap-stile in the wall on the left. Walk across the field towards Low Farm ahead, on the first horizon. Cross a footbridge and walk uphill; keep left of farm buildings, take a metal gate, and go right along a minor road. When the road bears right, and forks, walk left along a track (signed as a cul-de-sac) down to Ludburn Farm.

Cross the farmyard and continue down the track; at the bottom of the hill take a footbridge on the left across the River Manifold. Follow the wall ahead to join a hollow-way, uphill. 50m before a collection of farm buildings, look out for a wall-stile on the left; from here you have easy level walking on a field-path punctuated by gap stiles.

Keep right of a barn, then left of Lower Boothlow Farm, to follow a path alongside a wall, signed to Longnor. A succession of field-stiles directs you closer to the river, before veering right, uphill, and through the yard of Folds End Farm. Continue uphill, on a farm-track, to arrive back in Longnor.

# THE ROBIN HOOD

BASLOW

*A fine ramble around gritstone crags and the tranquil parkland of Chatsworth Estate*

DISTANCE: 5 miles (8km)
ALLOW: 2¹/₂ hours
MAP: OS Outdoor Leisure 24
TERRAIN: Easy
PARKING: Free public car-park adjacent to the pub's own car-park

The Robin Hood can be found on the A619, two miles (3km) east of Baslow. The Robin Hood's public bar is called the Hikers' Den, where dogs and walking boots are welcome. A wide range of food is available from 11.30am-2pm every day, plus specials chalked up on a board. Tel: 01246-583186.

Walk right along the main A619 in the direction of Baslow. After just 50m take a stile on the left; a fingerpost indicates this is a permissive path to Baslow. This first part of the walk takes you through the Chatsworth Estate. Take steps down to a basic wooden footbridge over Heathy Lea Brook; afterwards keep right as the path forks, cross a stony track, and continue uphill to a ladder-stile.

The path continues uphill, at the back of a series of gritstone crags known as Dobb Edge. The path is easy to follow, via wooden and gap-stiles, along the edge of the ridge, down to a step-stile in a high wall. Bear right to follow a grassy hollow-way downhill, before heading left (there's no distinct path) across the parkland. Keep well left of the Estate's gatehouses; when your progress is stopped by a fence, follow it around to the left and through a metal kissing gate in a wall. Follow a track past a thatched cottage and a three-arched stone bridge to arrive in Baslow.

*A little of Chatsworth's gentility seems to have rubbed off on Baslow. This part of the village, known as Nether End, boasts thatched cottages (a rarity in the Peak), a 17th century arched bridge and a diminutive toll-house, all grouped around the northern entrance to the Chatsworth Estate.*

(*) Cross the triangle of grass – known as the Goose Green – at the traffic lights, and walk up Eaton Hill, immediately to the right of Il Lupo Italian restaurant. At the top, bear right, uphill, along Bar Road (signed as a cul-de-sac). When the houses peter out, the road

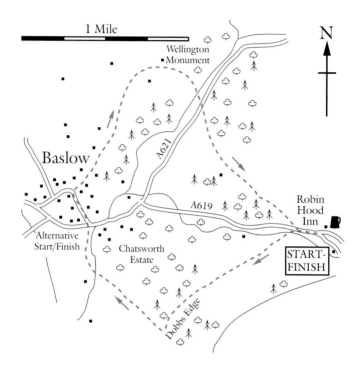

becomes a stony track between walls. After about 800m you emerge through a gate into open country. Leave the track here, and take a path to the right, alongside a wall.

*The view opens up to the right, back over Baslow, the Chatsworth Estate and the River Derwent. Ahead of you, perched on top of Baslow Edge, is Wellington's Monument: a sturdy cross erected in 1866 to complement the monument to Nelson, sited just a mile away on Birchen Edge.*

You have level walking through a landscape of bracken,

rocks and scattered trees, before descending through thicker woodland. When the wall on your right heads straight downhill, your path accompanies it through a birch wood. Take a stile and steps by a house, and follow a ginnel down to an old packhorse bridge spanning Bar Brook.

Follow a path uphill, emerging through a gate onto the A621; cross the road and take a stile to the left of Cupola Cottage. Another stile at the back of the house gives access to a path that follows a fence uphill.

The path soon levels out onto the breezy, bracken-covered 'tops', with gritstone edges to your left and expansive views to your right. Soon you can see your destination, the Robin Hood pub, straight ahead in the valley. The path makes a beeline for it; when you come down to a stile on the main A619 road the pub is only 100m away.

# THE MINERS' ARMS

*A mere stroll from a historic village, to whet the appetite or walk off a meal*

DISTANCE: 3 miles (5km)
ALLOW: 1¹/₂ hours
MAP: OS Outdoor Leisure 24
TERRAIN: Easy
PARKING: Pay and display car-park at the eastern end of Eyam (signposted from the Square in the centre of village)

The Miners' Arms, being hidden from Eyam's main street, is not the easiest of pubs to find. If you stand in the Square, look between a pair of shops for Water Lane and the 17th century pub, which pre-dates, by 30 years, the outbreak of the plague. Walkers are welcome provided they remove muddy boots. Bar meals are served from 12-2pm every day; the restaurant is open daily from 7-9pm. Tel: 01433-630853.

*This short walk should leave you plenty of time to explore this fascinating little village, whose inhabitants withstood the bubonic plague of 1665 with such bravery and fortitude. The virus is thought to have been carried in a box of cloth delivered from London to a travelling tailor. He was the first to succumb, followed rapidly by many of the villagers.*

*Eyam's young vicar, William Mompesson, is particularly remembered for encouraging the villagers to impose a quarantine upon themselves and thus prevent the disease from spreading. His selflessness, and*

*the tragic consequences for the 259 villagers who*
*succumbed to the plague, has kept Eyam's name fresh in*
*the memory. The significant buildings bear informative*
*plaques.*

From the Square in Eyam (pronounce it 'Eem' if you
want to sound like a local) take the road signed to
Hathersage, slightly uphill. As you leave the village, bear
left up a lane signed cul-de-sac and 'footpath to Riley
graves'. Walk up the lane, to find the long, raw gash of
Stoney Middleton Quarry dominating the view to the
right.

At the top of the hill, where the lane continues left to
Riley House Farm, your route is a stony track to the
right, again signed to the Riley graves. Soon you will see,

in a field on the left, what looks like a little sheep fold; you can take a stile to investigate it.

*This isolated group of graves is a poignant reminder of the plague years, with all seven graves belonging to the members of the Hancock family: the father, his three daughters and three sons. We can only imagine the torment of the woman who had to bury perhaps her entire family in this lonely spot.*

Continue along the track to reach woodland on your right. Follow a waymarker to take a path downhill, through the wood. When the path forks, keep right, downhill, through a gate. Continue in the same direction along a field path, keeping a wall to your left. You have views ahead over the valley of the River Derwent, with the steep-sided ridge of Froggatt Edge as a backdrop.

Meet a road, and cross it to take a walled track, downhill, passing a pair of tiny reservoirs, then woodland, before you join a metalled lane that meanders into the little village of Stoney Middleton. Dwarfed by the nearby quarry and hemmed in by vertiginous limestone cliffs, the village encourages few drivers on the A623 to take a closer look. But you will pass the unusual octagonal church of St Martin and a bath-house constructed around a spring whose waters might once have rivalled those at Buxton for their curative properties.

50m past the church, bear right up The Bank. At a 'no through road' sign bear right and immediately left, along a narrow lane signed Footpath to Eyam. After the last house on your left, look out for a stile on the left and join a field path waymarked Eyam $\frac{1}{2}$ mile. Walk steeply

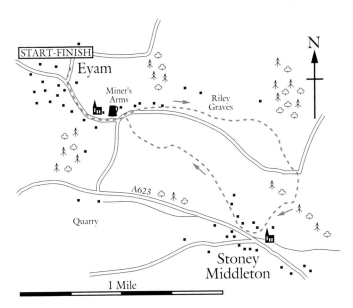

uphill; once you have crested the hill look out on your right for the Boundary Stone. The six holes in the top of the stone are supposed to be where coins, disinfected by vinegar, were left by the plague-ridden inhabitants of Eyam in exchange for goods.

After a gap-stile, follow a walled path; your route ahead is clear, through gates, to a farm. Join a little lane ahead to stroll back down into the Square at Eyam.

# LADYBOWER INN

*A high-level ridge walk boasting terrific views, with the return leg alongside the Ladybower Reservoir*

DISTANCE: 9 miles (15 km)
ALLOW: 4$^1$/$_2$ hours
MAP: Most of route on OS Outdoor Leisure 1, or use Landranger 110
TERRAIN: Moderate
PARKING: Free parking in the pub's large car-park

The Ladybower Inn, a free house enjoying splendid views across the Derwent Dam and Ladybower Reservoir, can be found on the A57 Snake Road between Sheffield and Glossop. Food from an extensive menu is available 12- 3pm, and 5-9pm, and there are tables on the front terrace. The licensees are happy for pub walkers to leave their cars in the pub's car-park. Tel: 01433-651241.

Cross the road from the car-park and take the path immediately to the right of the pub, uphill; after just 75 metres bear sharp left on another path that passes behind the pub, first through woodland then uphill through bracken. You quickly gain views on the left, down to Ladybower Reservoir.

*Early in the Second World War, the Lancasters of the famous Dambuster Squadron practised using the bouncing bombs at the reservoir, prior to destroying the Mohne and Eder dams in Germany's Ruhr Valley.*

Follow a wall; when the path forks, keep straight ahead, by the wall, and walk down to a pair of gates. Take a track, uphill, through a conifer plantation. The track soon levels off and follows first a fence and then a wall, as you leave the woodland behind and head up to the open moorland.

*The views are more extensive now, across the northern spur of Ladybower Reservoir and the other reservoirs – Derwent and Howden – that were created by flooding the Derwent*

*Valley. The project began at the turn of the century, submerging the villages of Derwent and Ashopton. Ladybower Reservoir was completed in 1943.*

Ignore minor paths crossing your route and keep following the wall until the path forks, almost beneath the rocky crag of Whinstone Lee Tor. Leave the wall and take the right fork, steeply uphill, to come to a meeting of tracks. Carry on up the hill, heading for a National Trust sign at the top. When you reach it you will be able to enjoy new panoramic views to the east, across Bradfield and Hallam Moors.

There's another junction of tracks here; your route is left, uphill, towards a stony crag (signed 'no access for cyclists'). At the top of the crag your way ahead becomes clear, as the full length of Derwent Edge comes into view – punctuated at intervals by a series of rocky outcrops, all of which you will visit.

Bear right on an unambiguous path along the ridge, to enjoy superb views to your left. Keep straight on when your route is crossed by another path, by a footpath sign. Pass the curiously weathered collection of rocks – almost a Henry Moore sculpture – known as the Wheel Stones. Then clamber over the rocks of White Tor. To see the almost symmetrical weathered obelisk known, not unreasonably, as the salt cellar, you will need to make a slight detour to your left at the next rocky outcrop.

After Dovestone Tor you pass to the left of a grouping of stones known, for obvious reasons, as the Cakes of Bread; at this point the peaty path, badly eroded in places, has been consolidated with heavy stone flags. Just

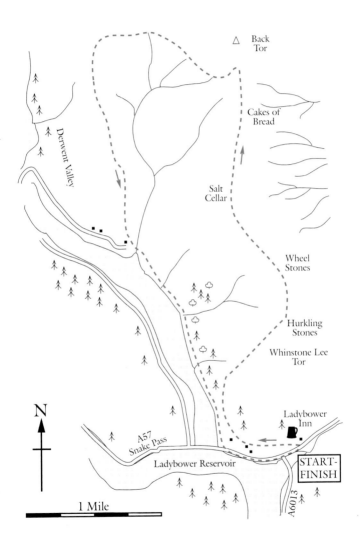

Back
Tor

Cakes of
Bread

Derwent Valley

Salt
Cellar

Wheel
Stones

Hurkling
Stones

Whinstone Lee
Tor

Ladybower
Inn

N

A57
Snake Pass

Ladybower Reservoir

A6013

START-
FINISH

1 Mile

*51*

100m from Back Tor, the highest point on the ridge, is a
meeting of tracks by an old waymarker stone.

Go left here to begin a long and gradual descent on a
path which, although not as broad as the ridge path, is
nevertheless easy to follow – through a bleak landscape of
heather and peat, with probably just a few red grouse for
company. The walking levels out after the path bears to
the left, with the reservoir coming back into view. Keep
left when the path forks, and almost immediately left
again at another fork, to follow a track slightly downhill,
soon crossing a line of grouse butts from which well-
heeled hunters send small game birds to meet their
Maker.

At a fingerpost you meet another track; go left here,
signed to Pike Low and Derwent. When the track forks
immediately afterwards, keep left towards another
fingerpost on the first horizon. Pass a small conifer
plantation (but ignore a path to it); keep straight ahead
at the fingerpost, and soon follow a tumble-down wall.

You have good level walking on a more substantial track,
now heading straight towards the reservoir. At a wall-end
and fingerpost, keep left, downhill, on a track. Negotiate
a ladder-stile and continue downhill to a farm. Take a
gate to the left of the farm, to follow a sunken path with
a wall to your left. At a meeting of paths take a stile
ahead, and continue down the sunken path, to meet an
unmade track by the reservoir.

Walk left, soon crossing Mill Brook on a bridge. Here,
until it was flooded to create the reservoir, was the little
village of Derwent. You have level walking for weary legs

now, with views across the water to the serried ranks of conifers on the opposite bank.

Walk though deciduous woodland till, at a gate near the road-bridge across the reservoir, you reach the A57. You now have a little road-walking to the left, to bring you back to the Ladybower Inn.

# THE GEORGE

*The many delights of Dovedale from one of the Peak's 'picture postcard' villages*

DISTANCE: 4 miles (7km)
ALLOW: 2$^1$/$_2$ hours
MAP: OS Outdoor Leisure 24
TERRAIN: Easy. Dovedale can get very crowded at weekends
PARKING: There is a small, free car-park (with toilets) in the village; if full, park near the village green

Alstonefield lies towards the national park's southern boundary, two miles west of the main A515 road between Buxton and Ashbourne. The George, overlooking a green and fringed by trees, looks like every village pub should look. It's still the focal point of a pretty little village which once hosted an important market, and cattle sales were held at the George within living memory.

Inside there are cosy bars, with low beamed ceilings, and a dining room. Outside there are tables. Food is available every day, 12-2pm and 7-9.30pm; a homely touch is that you order your meals at the kitchen door. Tel: 01335-310205.

Leave Alstonefield on the road signposted to Wetton and Dovedale. Keep right, almost immediately, at a T-junction. Bear left soon after at another T-junction close to the village school and take a track to your left, between walls. After 150m the walled track goes right, but you keep straight on, through a gate, to follow an indistinct field path alongside a wall to your right.

At a solitary tree, bear half-right, as the walls close in to meet at a stile. Continue steeply downhill, following the wall, to meet a minor road in Hopedale. Cross it and take the walled track opposite, uphill (if it's April, your route will be lined with daffodils).

The track levels out as it approaches the cluster of farms that is Stanshope and becomes a metalled road. Pass a handsome farmhouse with a Georgian facade to arrive at a T-junction. Your route is acute left here, down a stony track. After just 100m take a stile in the wall to your

right, following a waymarker signed to Dovedale. Bear slightly left across a field, to take another wall stile, as your way ahead becomes clear: into steep-sided Hall Dale. At the next-but-one stile, don't cross; bear left here, into the valley, following a wall to your right.

After a couple more stiles you are enclosed by the limestone scenery of Hall Dale, which is now looked after by the National Trust. You have easy walking through this delightful dry valley, soon having a conifer plantation occupying the steep slope to your right. The landscape becomes more dramatic, with limestone scars towering above, as the valley opens up to the prospect of Dovedale itself.

The stony path descends steeply to the River Dove. Surrounded by gleaming limestone crags, this is a majestic sight at any time of the year. At the riverbank, go right, through a gap stile, and follow the river on a good path until you reach a footbridge overlooked by the limestone pinnacles of Ilam Rock and Pickering Tor. Cross the bridge, then bear left on an equally good track alongside the river, which bubbles lazily over a series of little (mostly man-made) ledges. The walking is easy, allowing you to enjoy the beautiful surroundings, as the valley opens up at Dove Holes.

Dove Holes was once a massive cave system carved out by glacial meltwaters; there are still caverns to explore. This splendid limestone landscape, now in the custody of the National Trust, has long been admired by such literary luminaries as Tennyson and Byron. Izaac Walton, author of *The Compleat Angler*, retained a special affection for the sparkling waters of the River Dove. This

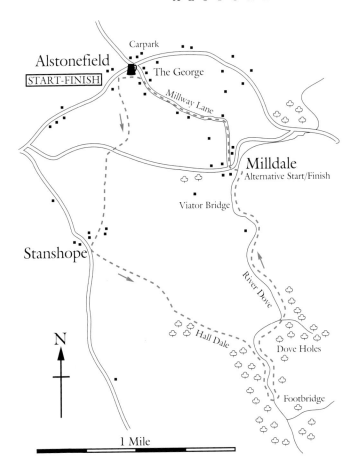

part of Dovedale is very popular; if it's holiday time you
won't be short of company. Keep following the river
upstream to reach another popular beauty spot.

*Milldale is a compact huddle of cottages shoehorned into
the valley bottom. The single stone arch of Viator's Bridge*

*was built for laden pack-ponies. A nearby barn has been
converted into a National Trust information point. The
barn was originally used to stable a pair of horses associated
with a cornmill, whose wheel was turned by water from the
River Dove. All that remains of the mill is the mill race,
sluice gate and the millstone.*

(\*) Locate a narrow lane passing Polly's Cottage
(refreshments available here), known as Millway Lane.
It's marked as a cul-de-sac, but not for walkers, who have
a short, stiff climb to return to Alstonefield by way of the
parish church.

# THE SHADY OAK

F E R N I L E E

*An easy circuit around Fernilee Reservoir and the wooded Goyt Valley*

DISTANCE: 5 miles (8km)
ALLOW: 2¹/₂ hours
MAP: OS Outdoor Leisure 24
TERRAIN: Easy
PARKING: Pub walkers are welcome to park in the pub's own car-park

The Shady Oak, with a Victorian postbox inset into its facade, enjoys a splendid situation overlooking the reservoirs of the Goyt Valley. You will find it on the A5004, just two miles (3.5km) south of Whaley Bridge. The extensive menu is chalked up on a blackboard and meals are available 11.30am-2.30pm (Sundays 12-2.30pm) and 7-9pm. The pub has its own little leaflet that describes a number of walks from here. Tel: 01663-732212.

*The Goyt Valley gets very busy at peak times; a problem exacerbated by the narrowness of the minor roads that twist and turn around the southern end. This walk, however, will keep you well away from traffic congestion, and allow you explore the best way, on foot.*

Cross the main A5004 road and take the track opposite, walking down to – and across – a large farmyard. Take a stile at the far side, bearing slightly left across a field to meet another stile. Continue downhill across the next field; with no detectable path, look out for a wooden footbridge

over a tiny beck. Further downhill, cross the River Goyt
on a more substantial footbridge, and immediately take
the left of two stiles to cross yet another footbridge. This
is a lovely spot, at the meeting of becks; mature
deciduous trees make an ideal habitat for birds such as
treecreepers and woodpeckers.

Join a good track uphill, away from the river, towards
Knipe Farm. Keep left of the farmhouse and follow a
wall for 100m, before taking a gate in this wall. Walk
uphill for just 20m, and go right, along a farm track,
around the front of Knipe Farm. Ignore a footpath
immediately after the farm which heads into woodland.
Your route is 30m further on: through a gate (a sign
indicates that you are joining the Midshires Way), and

uphill on a field path, keeping the wood to your left.

You are now walking up a pleasant little side valley called Mill Clough. After a gate you meet a track and follow it to the left, uphill, passing farm buildings. Soon the track levels out, offering wide views across the the Goyt Valley.

*The valley has changed beyond recognition in the last 50 years, with Stockport Corporation damming the River Goyt to create two reservoirs: first Fernilee in 1938, then Errwood, 30 years later. The River Goyt flows from south to north and eventually drains into the River Mersey at Stockport.*

Keep skirting woodland to arrive at the more substantial farm of Oldfield. Follow a track behind the farmhouse. At a fork of tracks bear right, uphill, on a stony track to a gate. Here you are entering Forestry Commission land, on a typically good track through a pleasing mixture of conifers (planted during the 1960s) and older broad-leaved trees. Once the trees have thinned out a little on your left, you can enjoy more valley views.

After about a mile (1.5km) on this track you meet a gate by a road. Don't go through the gate, but take instead a grassy path, acute left, that goes downhill between a wall and a fence (a sign reads Fernilee Reservoir). After 50m the path bears right and follows a wooded clough downhill.

At a divergence of tracks, keep right, across a stile, to follow a wall down towards the water of

*61*

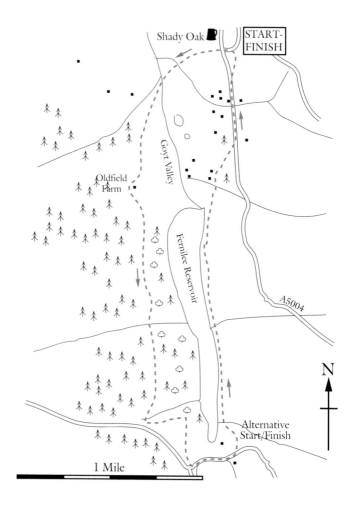

Shady Oak

START-FINISH

Goyt Valley

Oldfield Farm

Fernilee Reservoir

A5004

N

Alternative Start/Finish

1 Mile

Errwood Reservoir. This grassy track brings you out at
the road across the top of the dam. Cross the dam; at the
far side (*) take a metalled track down to the water of
Fernilee Reservoir (another path, easy to follow, cuts out
the walk over the dam). Beyond a kissing gate your track
becomes stony, and accompanies the water's edge for a
mile (1.5km).

After the reservoir dam, take a track – now metalled – as
it bends right, then left, and up through woodland, to
meet the main A5004 road. Walk left for just 150m, then
take a minor road on the right. 100m beyond a brick-
built chapel, bear sharp left down a narrow lane, to arrive
back at The Shady Oak.

# THE GROUSE INN

*A stroll along the gritsone escarpments of Froggatt Edge and White Edge, with superb views every step of the way*

DISTANCE: 7 miles (12km)
ALLOW: 3 hours
MAP: OS Outdoor Leisure 24
TERRAIN: Easy, mostly level walking
PARKING: Lay-by near the pub

You can find the Grouse Inn on the B6054, about 3 miles (5km) north of the village of Calver. From its solitary position at the northern end of Froggatt Edge, the pub enjoys enviable views across the Derwent Valley. Walkers with muddy boots and rucksacks are asked to enter the pub by the patio entrance at the back. The cosy bar is decorated with local photographs. Food is available on weekdays (except Monday & Tuesday) 12-2.30pm and 7-9.30pm, and weekends 12-3pm and 7-9.30pm. Many meals have been named after local places so you can enjoy dishes such as Stanedge Steak Pie and even (groan) Chinley-Con-Carne! Tel: 01433-630423.

Walk just 50m downhill from the pub, take a stile on the right between hedgerows, and join a field-path. Walk half-left across the field, through gate-posts, and half-left across the next field, too, to take a wooden gate in a wall.

Bear immediately left through Hay Wood: delightful deciduous

woodland. Cross a tiny beck and walk uphill to meet the road. Walk right, down the road, for 75m, then take a gate on the left and join a stony track uphill. Extensive views open up on the right – to the west – as the track levels out through more broad-leaved woodland.

*Froggatt Edge is a long gritstone escarpment, which offers both excellent walking along the top as well as a challenge for rock-climbers. As the woodland thins out, the view becomes more expansive, towards Grindleford and Stonehall Quarry. The village of Stoney Middleton – wedged into its narrow valley and surrounded by limestone quarries – soon comes into view, and the moorland beyond. To the left, too, is open heather moorland extending to the immediate horizon, which is dominated by the less dramatic length of White Edge (your return route).*

No route-finding instructions are needed: just keep to the path that follows the edge (the southern section being known as Curbar Edge) until you come to a wooden kissing gate. Follow a wall ahead to reach Curbar Gap car-park (pay & display), an alternative start for the walk. Curbar Gap is a depression between the outcrops of Curbar Edge and nearby Baslow Edge that allowed a road to be built to link the villages in the valley with Sheffield to the east.

(*) From the car-park, walk left to locate a gate and stile by the road, just 10m from an old waymarker stone whose inscribed directions are now almost indecipherable. Join a track ahead that follows a wall. After 100m, when both track and wall turn sharp left, take a track to the right across rough pasture. You soon meet and follow a wall down to a flat wooden bridge over a boggy area, then uphill. When the wall goes left, at a junction of tracks, follow it for just a few metres (a waymarker post indicates Longshaw) before climbing to the top of White Ridge.

Again, you have few route-finding problems from here; just keep to the path along White Ridge, through an open landscape of heather moorland, grassy pasture and scattered trees.

White Ridge has none of the rocky outcrops which typify Froggatt and Curbar Edges. To the right is the

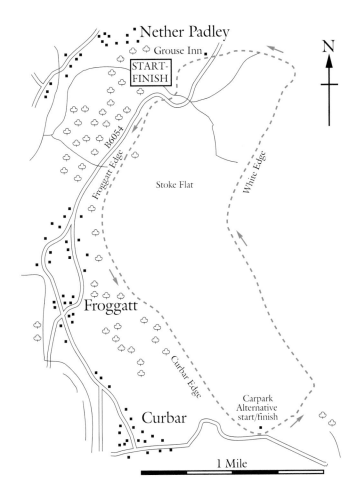

untrodden expanse of Big Moor. Towards the northern end of White Ridge is a rocky outcrop known as the Bullet Stones.

Walk about 300m further to go through a gap in a wall, and bear left to follow the wall (waymarked to The Grouse Inn). The path leads downhill into coppiced woodland; follow another fingerpost to leave the wood via a gate, and follow a field path back to The Grouse Inn.

# THE OLD NAG'S HEAD

E D A L E

*A classic encounter with gritstone and a chance to rub shoulders with Pennine Way-farers*

DISTANCE: 6 miles (11km)
ALLOW: 3½ hours
MAP: OS Outdoor Leisure 1
TERRAIN: Moderate, but a long climb for the first section of the walk
PARKING: Pay & display car-park in Edale

The Old Nag's Head is a free house that dates from 1577, when the customers would include the drivers of packhorse teams, transporting goods across the Pennines. The Hikers' Bar has a tiled floor, low-beamed roof and a roaring log-fire. The food is as hearty as you'd expect from a pub that is the official start of the Pennine Way. Meals are served from 12-3pm, 6-9pm (Sundays 12-7pm) Tel: 01433-670291.

*Edale is the gateway to the desolate wilderness of Kinder Scout. Many Pennine Way-farers progress no further, becoming weary and disillusioned by the boggy terrain. Reluctant bog-trotters can be reassured, however, that the Kinder plateau can best be explored along its perimeter, of which this splendid walk is merely a part.*

*For all its popularity, being one of the few villages in the Peak directly accessible by rail, Edale panders little to the tourist trade. Primarily a walker's centre, the village seems to cope with the veritable army of serious, cagoule-clad ramblers. This walk offers a flavour of*

*the dramatic landscape, without the chance of getting lost.*
*Nevertheless, ensure you have adequate wet-weather gear,*
*as the weather conditions can change rapidly.*

From the car-park bear right along the road, beneath the
railway bridge, into Edale village. Continue past The Old
Nag's Head, as the road soon becomes a stony track.
When it turns into a private drive, your route is to the
right, signed footpath to Grindsbrook. Cross a log bridge
over Grindsbrook, then join a path uphill (unmissable as
it's stone-flagged). This is the beginning of the Pennine
Way.

Just after a small barn-like building on the left, you leave
the 'yellow brick road', to take a path that strikes off to
the right, uphill, towards a small conifer plantation. Meet

a stile at the top of the field and continue up stone steps. The steepness of the climb ensures that just a few minutes out of Edale you can enjoy splendid views south across to Mam Tor and the ridge walk; and north to the ridge you'll soon be exploring.

When the path forks, keep right (signed footpath to Nab). You soon reach the Nab – a good viewpoint – but your path continues to zig-zag uphill, giving sight of your immediate target: a rocky outcrop called Ringing Roger. A path heads off to the top of Ringing Roger (a bit of a scramble near the top); the easier option is to keep left of the outcrop, on a good path that climbs inexorably up to the skyline.

*The steep-sided Grindsbrook valley is shaped like an inverted triangle, with Edale village at the base, and this walk divides naturally into three sections. The first is the long ascent you have nearly completed; the second offers easy, high-level walking along the top of the ridge; the third comprises the gradual descent back into Edale. So your immediate aim is the top right-hand corner of that triangle.*

The path takes you around the head of Golden Clough (there's a little beck to jump across), to begin the level walk along the top of the valley, passing the gritstone outcrop of Nether Tor. The path ahead is easy to follow, enabling you to enjoy the extensive views. The path stays close to the lip of the valley, except for a few boggy areas, where you have to make minor detours to stay dry. Once you reach the outcrop of Upper Tor, the highest point on this walk, you get views to the north, across the Woodlands Valley.

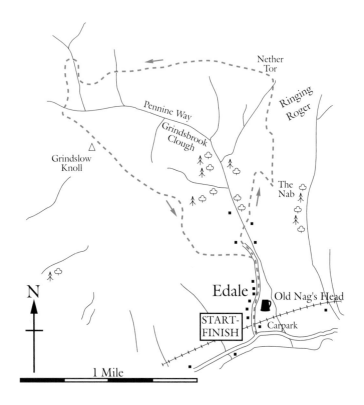

As you approach Grindsbrook Clough the path bears right, to take you around a dramatic ravine, before doubling back to head for the prominence of Grindslow Knoll. Soon you cross the route of the Pennine Way; having first walked and then clambered up Grindsbrook Clough. Pennine Way-farers now head off towards the Kinder Downfall. But your route is straight on, passing a curiously weathered rock (called the Anvil Stone, but bearing more than a passing resemblance to ET's head).

A choice of paths gives you the option of reaching the top of Grindslow Knoll, or skirting the left flank. Either way, the paths soon rejoin for the long descent towards Edale in the valley bottom. Quite steep and rocky at first, the path descends to a stile, after which you walk on grass. This field-path wheels left and is soon enclosed by hedgerows. You join the alternative Pennine Way route, to follow a stream back down into Edale, directly opposite The Old Nag's Head.

# BARREL INN

*An easy stroll by wood and water, from the splendid viewpoint of Eyam Edge*

DISTANCE: 4 miles (7km)
ALLOW: 2 hours
MAP: OS Outdoor Leisure 24
TERRAIN: Easy
PARKING: On the grass verges near the pub

You will search in vain for the village of Bretton, since it comprises merely the Barrel Inn, a couple of adjacent farmhouses and a Youth Hostel. The pub is more or less equidistant from the villages of Great Hucklow, Foolow and Eyam. From Foolow there is a road (signed to Bretton) which takes you straight to the pub.

The Barrel Inn has been a landmark on Eyam Edge since the early years of the 17th century. From this vantage point, at least 450m above sea level, the views are stunning – the prime pastoral landscape between the villages of Foolow and Eyam, divided up neatly by dry-stone walls. Low ceilings and an open fire give the pub a homely feel. The menu is supplemented by daily specials; meals available 12-2.30pm and 6.30-9pm. Tel: 01433-630856.

Take a minor road immediately to the left of the pub, to enjoy lovely views over farmland. After a mile you come to a house on the left; follow the fingerpost here (footpath to Abney) immediately to the right of the house (don't worry, it's a right of way). Walk downhill, keeping a field-wall to your left. Cross a stile and bear slightly right to pick up a path, steeply downhill, through scrubland.

After a gap-stile in a fence you have a bit of a scramble steeply downhill into a hummocky landscape. Follow the

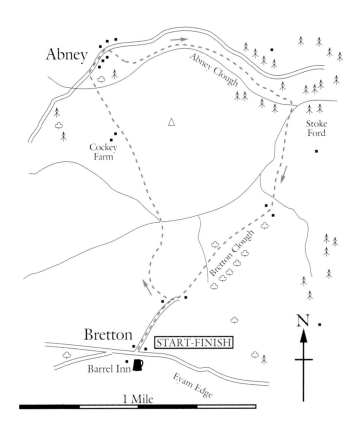

path down to a stream and cross on a wooden footbridge. Over a stile and another footbridge you climb steps uphill; your path soon rises above a wooded clough. When you leave the woodland behind you take a stile and follow a field-path to the right, hugging a wall. Follow the wall around to the left, take two more stiles, to keep right of Cockey Farm.

Join the farm track, but only until it wheels left beyond the farmhouse; here you follow a wall (and footpath sign) to the right, to head towards the village of Abney on the first horizon. When the wall curls to the right, follow it to take a gap stile. Go left (Abney sign) to cross a field, soon downhill, to step across a tiny beck. Ignore the grassy track ahead, and bear right to join a path, over a stile, and steeply down to a footbridge over another beck. Go steeply up to a road at the top.

Walk right, into the handful of houses that constitutes the hamlet of Abney. After just 200m of road walking, bear right, through a gate, onto a stony track (signed as a footpath via Stoke Ford to Eyam). Through another gate you have a grassy track to walk on, through scrubland, with a brook to your right. This scrubby habitat acts like a magnet for many kinds of woodland birds, including jay, wren, long-tailed tit, treecreeper ... perhaps even a green or greater spotted woodpecker.

Walk downhill after a pair of stone gate-posts and follow the beck; through a gate you find yourself in conifer woodland. Here you may catch a glimpse of a goldcrest, which vies with the wren to be Britain's smallest bird. Soon you come to Stoke Ford, a delightful spot and a meeting place of brooks and tracks.

Cross a pair of wooden footbridges, then bear right, uphill, signed to Gotherage Farm, Grindleford and Eyam.

After just 50m the track forks; keep on the right-hand track, climbing very gradually through a landscape of bracken, gorse and scattered trees. When your path bears right on an embankment, to cross another little beck, take an indistinct field-path ahead, steeply uphill, keeping a tumble-down wall to your left.

Soon you have easy, level walking before taking the left flank of a little side valley. Follow the path down to a stile, then steeply uphill on the opposite side of the valley. Keep climbing through woodland; where you leave the trees behind is a well-placed seat. The path continues up to a stile and then crosses a field to pass a house, now enclosed by walls. Meet a road and walk right; soon you will arrive back at the Barrel Inn.

# MONSAL HEAD HOTEL

MONSAL HEAD

*An exhilarating walk that starts and ends at one of the finest views in the Peak*

DISTANCE: 5 miles (8km)
ALLOW: 2¹/₂ hours
MAP: OS Outdoor Leisure 24
TERRAIN: Easy
PARKING: Pay & display car-park adjacent to the Monsal Head Hotel

The Monsal Head Hotel, on the B6465 north-west of Bakewell, enjoys a splendid setting, overlooking one of Derbyshire's most admired views. Walkers are welcome in the Stable Bar, behind the main hotel building, which is divided up into 'stable stalls' and decorated with horse 'tack'. Best of all is the big log fire. Hearty meals are now served all day, every day, from 12-9.30pm. Amongst the guest beers is Monsal Best Bitter, brewed specially for the hotel. Tel: 01629-640250.

Spread out below is the steep-sided and wooded valley of Monsal Dale, and the River Wye, which you accompany for most of this walk.

Stand overlooking the view; a trio of fingerpost signs show the walking options down into the valley below. Take the right-hand path, signed Monsal Dale, Trail & Viaduct. After a set of steps, go left and follow the path down to the trackbed of the old Midland Railway line.

*Parts of the old line are now being*

*promoted to walkers and cyclists as the Monsal Trail. John Ruskin's was one of the more vociferous voices to be raised when a plan was mooted to span the limestone valley with a 26m high railway viaduct. It was nevertheless built in 1867 and carried trains until the line was closed 100 years later. Now, of course, the viaduct and cuttings are bedded into the landscape; there would probably be just as many protesting voices raised if the viaduct were to be demolished!*

Cross the viaduct, then take a gate and path to the left, to enjoy level walking parallel to the River Wye, with the steep-sided, wooded flanks of Monsal Dale rising up on either side, topped with limestone crags. Soon you are on a broader track, closer to the river, as you pass a tall weir. Cross the tiniest of becks, then another (on stepping stones), to meet the main A6 road.

Cross the road into a car-park; take steps up to a stile and follow a well-defined field path ahead. Keep 'on the level' until, after a pair of stiles, you walk uphill, between rocky limestone outcrops. The path zig-zags uphill (a fingerpost reads Ashford) into Great Shacklow Wood. Cross a wall-stile; soon you have level walking through the woods, followed by a gradual descent. Keep straight ahead at a three-way fingerpost, skirting the bottom of a wood and passing fish-ponds, to approach the River Wye once again.

Beyond a weir there is a long-abandoned mill race feeding the twin water-wheels of a handsome little mill, by an old stone bridge. Don't cross it, but keep straight ahead on the path that accompanies the meandering river. Go left when you reach a minor road, then right as you meet the main A6 again. As you approach Ashford village, cross the River Wye on a three-arched bridge.

*This is Sheepwash Bridge, on an old packhorse trail. Sheep were brought here to be washed before they were sheared; a holding pen can be seen on the side of the bridge nearest the road.*

*Ashford in the Water (to give it its 'Sunday best' name) is one of the most attractive villages in the Peak. It was a centre of lead mining until the end of the last century, after which the mining and working of Ashford 'black marble' (enjoying a vogue for jewellery) helped to bolster the local economy.*

Walk up Fennel Street, passing a grassy area with a seat,

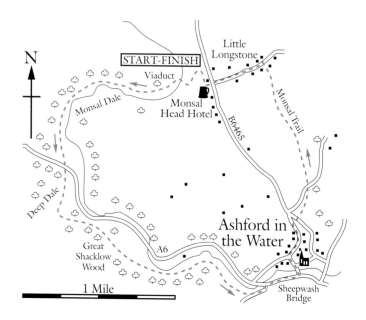

and continue up Vicarage Lane (signed to Monsal Head and Wardlow). Once you have left the village behind, take a gap stile on the right, signed as a footpath to Monsal Head. Cross a field to a stile, cross a road and take a path to the left of a barn. This field-path follows a wall uphill. Pass behind a farm, continuing through a succession of gap-stiles, until you reach a railway trackbed. Cross it (no need to worry about trains any more) and, after a stile, go left along a field-path.

Veer right past a gate and head towards a group of houses on the immediate horizon. The next two gates can't be left open by even the most thoughtless of

walkers, thanks to a pair of large stone counterweights.
Stroll through parkland to reach the hamlet of Little
Longstone. Walk left along the road, passing a pub called
the Packhorse; it's quite a surprise when you crest the hill
and find yourself back at the Monsal Head Hotel
overlooking that gorgeous view.

# CASTLE INN

BAKEWELL

*A walk through woodland and along the River Wye from the bustling town of Bakewell*

DISTANCE: 5¹/₂ miles (9km)
ALLOW: 3 hours
MAP: OS Outdoor Leisure 24
TERRAIN: Easy
PARKING: There are a number of pay & display car-parks in Bakewell, with the cheapest being just over the river bridge

Just a few metres from the splendid stone bridge over the River Wye, the 16th century Castle Inn has been refurbished. With its stone-flagged floors the pub is now more user friendly and a good selection of meals cater for the heartiest appetite. Food is served during the week between 11.30am-2.30pm and 6.30-8.30pm; Saturday 11.30am-9pm; Sunday 12-8pm. Finish off with the town's speciality, but call it Bakewell *pudding* rather than *tart*. There are tables outside. Tel: 01629-812103.

*To exclude major towns and some of the more unsightly quarries, the boundary of the national park makes some exaggerated loops. This leaves the compact market town of Bakewell as both the national park's largest settlement and the site of its administrative offices. The River Wye meanders peacefully through the town and hungry ducks eat visitors' bread by the medieval bridge.*

If you start from the Castle Inn, cross the river bridge and take Station Road, the first road on the right and signposted Industrial Estate. Go immediately right again, along Coombs Road, passing the car-park that is most convenient for this walk. After 100m go right, into another car-park. Walk to a gate at the far end; a footbridge over a mill-race gives access to the town centre, but your route is to the left instead, on a sandy track which skirts the showground. Bakewell Agricultural Show remains one of the largest in the country.

A gate beyond the showground gives access to a field-path; keep following a tall hedgerow to your left through successive fields, soon accompanying the river on one of

its slow meanders through the low-lying meadow. Cross a tiny beck on a footbridge and follow the river through a copse. Soon you leave the river on a well-defined field-path, passing an ancient tree that's almost split down the middle.

Meet a minor road (if you want to continue on to Haddon Hall, bear right along the road for just 30m, and follow a waymarked riverside path to the left). Otherwise bear left, up the road; as you make a sharp left-hand bend you are crossing a railway track-bed that has now become the Monsal Trail, a resource for walkers and cyclists. 100m beyond the bend, go right, through a gate (signed Bridle Road). Follow a field-path and wrought-iron fence around to the right, to meet a gate at the field corner. Keep following the fence, enjoying broadening views to the right over the Haddon Hall Estate. At the perimeter wall of Bowling Green Farm, take a track, to the left and uphill, to keep the farm to your right.

Follow the track as it is soon fringed by neatly-clipped hedges. At a junction of tracks about half a mile (1km) beyond the farm, keep left to get a long view up the valley towards Bakewell, and come down to a crossing of tracks. Your route is to bear half-left, on a good track up into woodland (signed footpath to Chatsworth).

Walk up through broad-leaved woodland, ignoring a track joining from the right. 70m further on, the track forks again; your route is to the right, following a blue arrow by a sign explaining you are on one of the Haddon Hall Estate's concessionary paths. Climb steeply up through conifers, soon getting long views over Bakewell

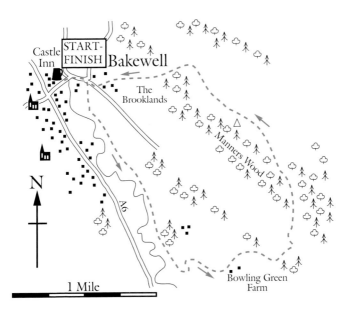

through a gap in the trees.

As you approach a smaller spur of the plantation, the track bears right, between stone gateposts, and narrows to a pleasant woodland path. At a gate in a wall, bear right, to cross a ladder-stile. Here is another choice of routes; the more obvious path is straight ahead, but your route is to the left, to skirt the conifer woodland on an indistinct field-path. To your right a new view presents itself: down over the Chatsworth Estate.

At the end of the plantation, strike off across the middle of a field towards a gate and stile on the first horizon, then across an even larger field in the same direction. The path becomes more obvious and leads you down to a gate in a fence, close to a pond. Go through the gate and bear half-left in front of a clump of trees. Walk down the field to locate a ladder-stile in a wall.

Take a path steeply downhill through woodland. When the path divides, go left, and immediately right, to continue downhill. At the bottom of the wood you have to cross a fairway of the Bakewell Golf Club, heading towards the town below. Over a ladder-stile, follow a grassy track across a railway trackbed (now the Monsal Trail).

Follow a hedge, and then a wall, to the left, to join a metalled track downhill that meets Coombs Road opposite the showground. Turn right to find yourself back in Bakewell.

# FARMYARD INN

*A n intimate exploration of Lathkill Dale, one of the Peak's most delectable valleys*

DISTANCE:
$7^1/_2$ miles (13 km)
ALLOW: $3^1/_2$ hours
MAP: OS Outdoor Leisure 24
TERRAIN: Easy
PARKING: Free car-park just 50 metres from the pub (further out of Youlgreave village)

The Farmyard Inn is a free house; its friendly bar has exposed beams, log fire and food every lunchtime (12-2pm) and evening (7-10pm). There are guest beers to supplement the Mansfield ales and no jukeboxes or one-arm bandits. There is a small beer garden. Tel: 01629-636221.

*Youlgreave is a handsome linear village just to the south of Bakewell. No fewer than five wells are dressed here each summer and you can still see the circular water tank made of stone – known locally as the fountain – which was erected in 1829 by the Youlgreave Friendly Society of Women to store the village's water supply.*

From either pub or car-park, turn right along the road. Walk uphill out of the village, keeping right at a road fork. Just past a barn, take a stile on the right (signed Limestone Way), and bear left, uphill, over two stiles. Then go through a gate to follow a wall on a level path.

Pass a picnic site and car park to a road; go left here. Take a stile by a fork in the road, and bear left across a field in the direction pointed by a fingerpost. The way ahead is clear: a field-path over stiles, through a copse, to Calling Low Farm. A succession of gates directs you to the right, around the farm, before you bear right, across a field towards another farm, with views of Lathkill Dale opening up to the right.

At a kissing gate is a sign from English Nature, welcoming you to Lathkill Dale. Go steeply downhill – steps have been made – into the dry valley of Cales Dale. After a stile at the bottom, join a path to the right. A beck emerges from almost beneath your feet, as you

arrive in the main limestone valley of Lathkill Dale.

*The River Lathkill is a clear and sparkling watercourse that teems with fish, aquatic life and a variety of water-loving birds such as the yellow wagtail, dipper and the metallic blue kingfisher. Izaak Walton, author of The Compleat Angler, considered the Lathkill to be "the purest and most transparent stream that I ever yet saw". Much of Lathkill Dale is now designated as a nature reserve, to preserve the delicate ecological balance of this beautiful valley.*

Go right after a footbridge to follow the River Lathkill; this is your path for about the next three miles (5km). Pass a pretty little waterfall (Pudding Springs), a weir (by the side valley of Twin Dales) and a mill race that once supplied water to the waterwheel of a long demolished mill. Pass the bases of pillars of what was once an aqueduct, which carried water to the Mandale Lead Mine.

*The sylvan delights of Lathkill Dale give only the slightest hints that the valley was, for centuries, exploited for lead ore. In 1836, a huge waterwheel, with a diameter of 17m, was built, in a doomed attempt to drain the deeper mines. Since then most of the workings have gone 'back to nature'.*

Pass a couple of caves to arrive at Lathkill Lodge, close to a little clapper bridge. Keep to the riverside here (a signpost directs you towards Conksbury). The river broadens after a set of weirs, as you reach a road at Conksbury Bridge (notice how small the bridge arches are). Cross the bridge and walk along the road for just 100m, before taking a path, left, to continue walking parallel to the River Lathkill. Your path follows a wall, crosses a track, and continues ahead: easy, grassy walking

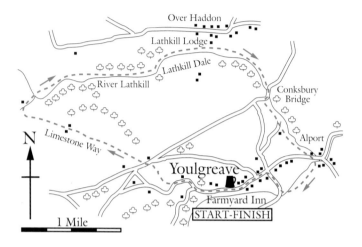

over a succession of stiles until you arrive in the little knot of buildings that comprises Alport.

Cross the road by a rather handsome farmhouse, and pick up a track ahead where the rivers Lathkill and Bradford meet. You have level walking beside the River Bradford through a delightful little valley. Pass a substantial bridge, cross the river and take a path uphill. Continue uphill to join a road, which takes you back into Youlgreave.

# YE OLDE ROYAL OAK
## W E T T O N

*The River Manifold flows (sometimes) through a wooded limestone valley, best explored from the trackbed of an old railway line*

DISTANCE: 6 miles (10 km)
ALLOW: 3 hours
MAP: OS Outdoor Leisure 24
TERRAIN: Easy; some walking on minor roads
PARKING: Free parking (and toilets) in car-park just 100m from the pub (turn right out of pub, and first right again)

Ye Olde Royal Oak – the home of the official World Toe Wrestling Championship – offers a warm welcome to walkers; there is even a rack where rucksacks can be stowed. You will find hearty meals every lunchtime (till 2pm) and evening, a selection of cosy bars and a beer garden. Tel: 01335-310287.

Wetton is an unpretentious little village, with few features to delay your walk. So turn right out of the car-park, along a minor road. Keep straight ahead, following the sign: Grindon & Manifold Valley. The road soon goes downhill, as you get views of the Manifold Valley and beyond. Go right at the T-junction; after a couple of hairpin bends you reach the River Manifold. Cross it on a single-arched stone bridge, and turn right into a car-park. (*) Continue straight ahead along a well-made track: easy, level walking, with the river to your right, and wooded slopes to your left.

*This track is the old trackbed of the Leek and Manifold Light Railway, built to carry milk from a local dairy and to serve the Ecton copper mines. It opened in 1904, but was closed within 30 years. It is now promoted to walkers and cyclists as the Manifold Trail; despite its road-quality surface there is no right of way for cars or motor-bikes. The Manifold is a 'real' river only after rain; between Wetton Mill and the village of Ilam it has the disconcerting habit of disappearing underground. During the summer months the river can be nothing more than a stony bed.*

You pass beneath a towering limestone outcrop, on the opposite side of the river.

*A gaping hole in the cliff-face announces the entrance to Thor's Cave, from which many artifacts have been unearthed, indicating that the cave was occupied by man from the Stone Age to the Roman occupation.*

If you want to investigate the cave more closely, you must cross the river on a footbridge. Otherwise continue along the track, until you cross the river at a busy meeting of roads and paths, by a car-park. Take either of the minor roads ahead (how often can you say that?) to arrive very shortly at another meeting of roads. Cross the river on an old stone bridge, to reach Wetton Mill.

*For three centuries the local farmers brought their corn to be ground at Wetton Mill. The building, dating back to 1577, is now a farm in the good custody of the National Trust. There is a little cafe at the mill, and seats outside, if you want to sit and enjoy the comings and goings at this popular little spot.*

(*) Take a track to the left of the mill, up to Dale Farm. Walk through the farmyard (signed footpath to Back of Ecton) to join a track that goes uphill, through a pleasant little valley. When the track veers left, continue straight ahead – towards a distinctive hill called the Sugarloaf. A stony path climbs steeply up the left flank of the hill; at the top take a pair of adjacent stiles to follow a hedgerow to your right.

You have easy walking, slightly uphill, soon following a wall on your left – straight ahead towards Broad Ecton Farm. 100m before the farm, take a stile by a little pond and walk to the right, along a farm track. Lovely views begin to open up: a typical Peak landscape of rolling hills, fields and open pasture.

Walk down to a hairpin bend; take another farm track here, on the right, towards Lees Farm. After just 20m take a stile on the left, then another, to walk downhill

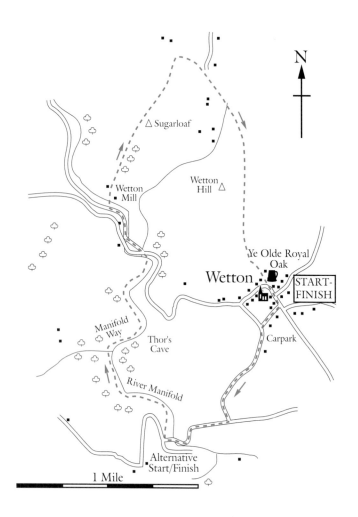

N

△ Sugarloaf

Wetton
Hill △

Wetton
Mill

Ye Olde Royal
Oak

Wetton

START-
FINISH

Manifold
Way

Thor's
Cave

Carpark

River Manifold

Alternative
Start/Finish

1 Mile

across a large field. Take a stile at the bottom, by a diminutive beck, then bear right to follow a track through open pasture that keeps left of Wetton Hill ahead. Continue uphill, and follow a wall, to take a stile near the top.

Bear left across the next field, keeping well to the left of a couple of barns, to find a stile in a fence. Follow a path uphill, and keep left of a system of field walls, to reach a wall-stile. Cross old quarry workings and follow a track back into the village of Wetton.

# PEEL ARMS

## PADFIELD

*A circuit of three of the reservoirs strung out along the Longdendale Valley*

DISTANCE:
6¹/₂ miles
(11km)
ALLOW: 3
hours
MAP: OS
Outdoor
Leisure 1
TERRAIN:
Easy
PARKING:
Limited street
parking in the
village of
Padfield, but
pub walkers are
welcome to use
the pub's own
car-park

The Peel Arms takes its name from Robert Peel, the man credited with creating the modern police force. Inside, the walls are rough-hewn stone, with every inch of shelf space crammed with decorative curios. Meals are served every day (except Sunday evenings): 12-2pm and 7-9pm. There is a small beer garden to the rear of the pub. Tel: 01457-852719.

Turn left out of the pub to arrive immediately at a T-junction. Go right, up the road, for just 50m, and take an unmade track to the left – beginning between houses numbered 117 and 127. Within seconds you've left Padfield behind to get views across the Longdendale Valley.

Walk down this good track for 500m, then take a stile on the left, cross a field and take another stile to meet a railway trackbed. Go right, along the sandy trackbed, which is being promoted as the Longdendale Trail (part of the longer Trans-Pennine

Trail) for use by walkers and cyclists. The views over the valley are extensive, except when you walk through a cutting and beneath a bridge.

Ignore a path leading down to the dam of Rhodeswood Reservoir and continue along the sandy track until you reach the main B6105 road. Bear sharp left here, onto a

road that soon takes you across the top of Torside
Reservoir's dam.

*Here you are joining the Pennine Way. The Longdendale
Valley is the end of a hard first day's walking across the
peat hags of Kinder. Crowden Youth Hostel, now just a
mile away, is a welcome sight for weary wayfarers.*

Where the Pennine Way continues up steps at the far end
of the dam, your route is to keep left, along the road.
Through a gate you join a concessionary path; your view
of the reservoir is filtered through conifer woodland.
When you come to the road that crosses the dam of
Rhodeswood Reservoir, go right, up the road to meet the
A628. Go left for 100m and cross the road (with care, as
this is a major trunk road for lorry traffic).

Take a substantial stony track, through a gate, and uphill
for 200m when, at a bridlepath sign, you bear slightly
left. Follow a grassy, level path, keeping a wall to your
left, that soon rises to another gate. The path, now
enclosed by walls, soon broadens – as do the views to the
left.

*The reservoirs of Longdendale are strung like a string of
beads along the valley. In a 30-year period from 1848, the
River Etherow was dammed to create five reservoirs. From
east to west they are Woodhead, Torside, Rhodeswood,
Valehouse and Bottoms.*

The walking is easy as you pass farm buildings and reach
the A628 once again. Walk right along the road, then,
after 200m, bear right along a minor road that takes you
into Tintwistle.

*Tintwistle lies on the western edge of the national park; for*

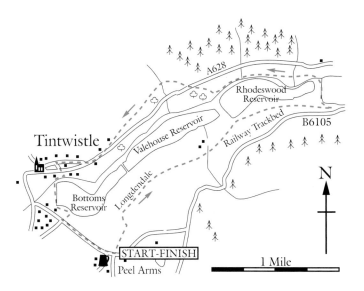

*travellers headed east, civilisation ends here. The village expanded, during the first half of the 19th century, with the success of the cotton industry. The water of the River Etherow powered a number of cotton mills, many years before the valley was flooded.*

Immediately before the car-park of the Bull's Head pub, go left down the cobbles of Chapel Brow. Cross the main road and walk left down a drive, signed as belonging to North West Water. When the road forks after 100m, keep right, through a metal gate, and follow a stony track down to the dam of Bottoms Reservoir. Walk across the dam, keeping to a grassy path at the top, following a wall. Bear left at the end of the wall; after 100m by the water's edge, take a stile in a wall on your right. Take steps uphill, to skirt a wood and emerge onto a road by a pub, the Victoria.

This is Padfield Main Road, and your route is left, to cover the 500m of fields that separates the communities of Hadfield and Padfield. On the way you cross the old railway line which occupied the first part of the walk, to arrive shortly back at the Peel Arms.

# CASTLE INN

C A S T L E T O N

*O*ne of the Peak's classic walks, along a ridge that affords expansive views in all directions

DISTANCE: 6½ miles (11 km)
ALLOW: 3½ hours
MAP: OS Outdoor Leisure 1
TERRAIN: Moderate
PARKING: Car-park (pay & display) almost opposite the Castle Hotel

The Castle Hotel, overlooked by the ruins of Peveril Castle, is all you could want after a ramble around this exhilarating ridge walk: cosy bars with stone-flagged floors, low beams, big log fires and oodles of character. The menu is supplemented by daily specials, chalked up on a board together with a 'useful fact of the day'. The people here look like they enjoy their work. There are seats outside for 'al fresco' drinking and dining. Tel: 01433 620578.

*Castleton is one of the national park's 'honeypot' villages and gets very crowded at holiday times. The attractions include four show caves open to the public, of which one – Speedwell Cavern – is explored by boat. These caverns were mined for minerals, particularly Blue John, a purple fluorspar. Peveril Castle, which gives the village its name, was built in 1076 by William de Peverel, one of William the Conqueror's favoured kinsmen.*

From the car-park, cross the road, and take a narrow lane signed Riverside Walk to Peak Cavern. A ginnel follows

a beck to another lane; go right here, crossing the beck
again, up Goosehill. Soon the lane becomes a stony track
with a high wall on the right. Through a gate you leave
the cramped back-streets of the village behind and
emerge into open grassland; follow a well-defined field-
path alongside a wall.

The landscape opens up to your right: a typical limestone
scene, with good views of Mam Tor and
the other hills surrounding Castleton.

It's easy walking till you meet the road by Speedwell Cavern. Walk left as the road, Winnats Pass, climbs steeply up between dramatic limestone crags.

At the top, immediately before a cattle grid, take a wall stile on the right, and walk at the back of Winnats Head Farm. Follow a wall and keep straight ahead at a three-way fingerpost, signed to Mam Tor.

Take a stile and cross a field to another stile; cross the road here and walk straight ahead on a field-path, towards the 'nick' on the near horizon. Cross another road to take a path steeply uphill; at the top, as you meet a road, (*) take steps on the right and follow the sign to Mam Tor. The way up to the top of Mam Tor has been stone-flagged.

*There are wonderfully expansive views from the top of Mam Tor: north to the Vale of Edale and the bleak moorland beyond, south towards Castleton set in a limestone landscape. Mam Tor (the name means 'the mother rock') comprises an unstable mixture of sandstone and shale. It is continually crumbling into the valley below and has already swept away the A625 road.*

Your route is obvious: a well-defined path along the ridge ahead, with the first section stone-flagged. There'll be time later on to relax in the pub and argue whether these stone flags are a necessary response to erosion of a popular footpath, or a bit of an eyesore.

Keep to the top of the ridge, enjoying the views to left and right; opposite a scar – Back Tor – the path

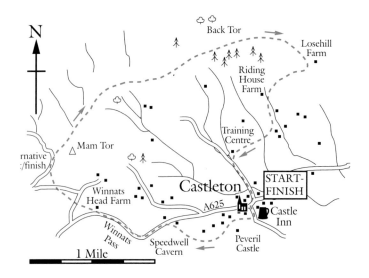

N

Back Tor

Losehill
Farm

Riding
House
Farm

Training
Centre

rnative
:/finish

△ Mam Tor

Castleton

START-
FINISH

A625

Winnats
Head Farm

Castle
Inn

Winnats
Pass

Speedwell
Cavern

Peveril
Castle

1 Mile

dips beneath the ridge-top to skirt a small conifer wood.
Beyond the wood, keep ahead on a field-path, slightly
uphill. Soon you have easy and level walking, with the
view of the vast Hope Cement Works becoming
increasingly dominant. Cross a few field-stiles; bear right
immediately before a stile sited near a pile of stones to
follow a fence downhill. Join a track to reach a fingerpost
at the back of Losehill Farm.

Bear right, downhill, signed to Castleton, and take a stile
at the field corner. Follow a wall down to another
fingerpost; go right here over pair of stiles and across a
field to join a rough farm track. At a meeting of tracks,
keep straight on, over a stile, to take a field-path
following a fence. After the next stile and a diminutive

beck, walk left, downhill, towards Riding House Farm.

Fifty metres before the farm buildings, look out for a fingerpost on the left, signed to Castleton, and follow a path along the right-hand edge of a field. Follow a beck steeply downhill, with steps down to cross the beck. Then keep left, now down the left-hand edge of the field, following the beck downhill to meet a track at the back of the National Park Study Centre. Turn right along this track, and follow it back into Castleton.

# BULL'S HEAD

M O N Y A S H

*The shorter of two walks that visit lovely Lathkill Dale; it can be combined with the Youlgreave walk to make a full-day's hike*

DISTANCE: 4 miles (7km)
ALLOW: 2 hours
MAP: OS Outdoor Leisure 24
TERRAIN: Easy
PARKING: Free car-park on Chapel Street, in the centre of the village

Monyash (with a probable meaning of 'many ash trees') has long been a self-sufficient little village, relying on farming, quarrying, rope-making and – most importantly – lead-mining. The market cross on the village green is a tangible reminder that the village was granted a market charter in 1340.

At one time there was enough business here to support five pubs. Now there is just one, the 17th century Bull's Head, which enjoys a lovely setting overlooking the village green. Weary walkers can enjoy their drinks in either of two bars, or on seats outside. Food, in portions to satisfy the hungriest of ramblers, is served from 12-2pm (12-2.30pm at weekends) and 7-9pm (6.30-9.30 at weekends). Tel: 01629-812372.

From either the pub or the car-park, walk to the far side of the green and take Rakes Road

(signed to Newhaven and Youlgreave). Pass Fere Mere:
the only survivor of five natural ponds that once supplied
the village livestock with water (another one was filled in
to make the car-park). When the road bears sharp right,
by a Georgian house (dated 1714), bear left on a farm-
track, and almost immediately left again, onto a stony
track between walls. After a pair of field-gates your route

**BULL'S HEAD**
...................................................................................................................

M  O  N  Y  A  S  H

is reduced to a footpath. When the path ends at a field, keep straight ahead following the wall to your right.

Opposite a National Trust sign (Fern Dale) take a wall-stile and follow a fingerpost across a field to a gap-stile. Now follow the wall to your left (a sign reads footpath to Youlgreave) over a step-stile.

At the next step-stile you cross the wall you have been following; now you keep it to your right. Go through a field gate to join a field-track to One Ash Grange Farm: it used to be an outlying grange – or farm – belonging to the monks of Roche Abbey, a once-thriving community in South Yorkshire.

The track goes between farm buildings and forks in front of a camping barn; bear left here and then soon right when it forks again (this little detour is merely to take you around the farmhouse).

Walk between a dutch barn and older outbuildings, to take a wall-stile. Join a field-path ahead to descend via stiles into Cales Dale; walk beneath a limestone cliff on your left down into the valley bottom. Keep ahead at a three-way fingerpost, through scrubland, and down to a wooden footbridge spanning the River Lathkill.

*The river has long been renowned for the clarity of its waters, and the variety of flora and fauna it supports. The grassy slopes of the upper valley are ablaze with colour each summer, with flowers such as Jacob's Ladder, trefoil and herb robert attracting a profusion of butterflies.*

Bear left immediately after the bridge, and walk up the valley, keeping the river to your left. These upper reaches of Lathkill Dale aren't as well wooded as the area

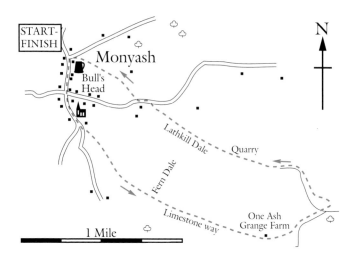

explored in the Youlgreave walk. But with its grassy slopes, rocky screes and limestone crags it is delightful nonetheless. Soon you come to Lathkill Head Cave: the bubbling source of the infant River Lathkill (except in dry seasons, when it emerges further down the valley).

Continue up the now-dry valley. Over a gap-stile the landscape becomes even more rocky. The stones come from nearby Ricklow Quarry, which used to be exploited for Derbyshire Marble. This was a type of limestone which, when polished, revealed intriguing patterns.

The limestone crags close in, making the valley almost grotto-like, as you negotiate a wooden kissing gate. Join a field-path; you have easy route-finding as the path emerges at a road.

Cross the road and follow a wall to the left, which leads you onto a path. Keep straight ahead, soon following a wall on your left. The route is easy to follow, via field-paths and wall-stiles, through the minor valley of Bagshaw Dale. At a road, walk left, and back up into Monyash.

# THE CHEQUERS INN

*A delight of a walk along the banks of the River Derwent, just long enough to raise an appetite*

DISTANCE: 3 miles (5km)
ALLOW: 1½ hours
MAP: OS Outdoor Leisure 24
TERRAIN: Easy
PARKING: Roadside parking opposite the pub

The Chequers Inn lies halfway up Froggatt Edge, on the B6054, just 2 miles (3km) north of Calver village. The bar has a wooden floor so walkers are welcome (though muddy boots should be left outside). There is a relaxed atmosphere and restrained decor to this old coaching inn. Meals range from sandwiches to more exotic fare, plus a full restaurant menu. Behind the pub is a delightful beer garden, surrounded by woodland. Bar meals are available Monday to Friday 12-2pm and 6-9.30pm; weekends 12-9.30pm. Tel: 01433-630231.

From the pub, walk downhill for just 75m, to take a gate on the right. Join a field-path downhill into woodland, and to a road. Walk right, still downhill; after 100m look for a step-stile in a wall on your left, giving access to a path alongside the River Derwent.

Go left to follow the river through delightful broad-leaved woodland: if it is summer you will enjoy a profusion of wild-flowers and songbirds. You

*113*

may cast an envious glance at some of the houses on your left, whose large gardens stretch almost down to the water.

At a handsome bridge – called New Bridge – take stone steps up to the road; cross the road to continue on the riverside path. Pass a broad weir, built to ensure a good head of water to supply power to Calver Mill. When you meet another road, walk right, to meet a road junction at the Bridge Inn, at the outskirts of Calver village.

Bear right, across the river bridge, and go right along a minor road immediately after a newsagent and general store. Pass Calver Mill and walk through stone gateposts (it is a right of way, for walkers at least), into a camp-site.

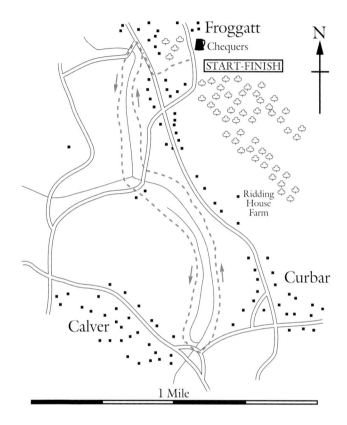

Froggatt

Chequers

START-FINISH

N

Ridding House Farm

Curbar

Calver

1 Mile

Pass an eccentric vernacular building with a bell-tower and stone columns supporting outside stairs that would not look out of place in a Roman forum.

Leave the camp-site via a kissing gate, and join a path through pasture land. The gritstone crags of Froggatt Edge dominate the horizon to the right: a rocky frieze against the skyline. You meet a watercourse: not, in fact, the Derwent, but a mill-leat that was built to bring water to the waterwheel of Calver Mill.

After a couple of bungalows you reach a road and New Bridge once again. Cross the road and take a gate, to continue walking by the riverside (making a little detour to cross a little beck on a footbridge). Reach the steep arch of Froggatt Bridge, and cross it; bear right immediately afterwards to take, after 150m, a stile on the left. Retrace your steps uphill, through scrubby woodland, to meet the B6054 road and The Chequers Inn.

# DEVONSHIRE ARMS

HARTINGTON

*A n easy circuit around three lovely dales, each with its own very individual character*

DISTANCE: 5¹/₂ miles (9km)
ALLOW: 3 hours
MAP: OS Outdoor Leisure 24
TERRAIN: Easy
PARKING: Free parking in the village of Hartington

The Devonshire Arms, named after the Duke of Devonshire whose influence was strongly felt in the area, occupies a prime spot in the village. The older part, to the right, is 16th century; the rest of the building, not as old, was originally used for storing goods being transported in and out of Hartington (you can still see the blocked-up archway used for horse-drawn carriages). Food is available all day in summer, from 12-9pm. During the winter months the times are 12-2.30pm and 7-9pm. Tel: 01298-84232.

*It is no surprise to learn that Hartington used to be a market town of some importance, as its handsome Georgian houses, shops and pubs are gathered around an extensive open area. Now, instead of market stalls, there is a collection of village greens and a duck pond.*

Turn right, outside the pub, along the Ashbourne road, and turn right immediately before a grey phone-booth and war memorial; the road is signed to the Youth Hostel. Walk uphill to pass the hostel, which provides an alternative use for the rather splendid manor house of Hartington Hall. Just 100m past the hostel, take a footpath sign on the right, through a metal gate. Bear left across a couple of fields (follow the direction of a waymarker), via gap-stiles, to approach a walled track. After 100m you can join the track, known as Highfield Lane, via another gap-stile. Walk uphill, passing a barn.

This is easy walking on a good track, hemmed in by limestone walls. Ignore paths forking first left, then right, to walk straight ahead between hawthorn trees.

You now have a narrower path leading downhill, to a trio of houses that comprises Dale End. Bear right at the road

for just 100m, then follow a footpath sign to the right. A sign announces you are approaching the Nature Reserve of Biggin Dale, well-known for its butterflies, summer flowers and gorse scrubland. Another good stony path leads downhill, passing a tiny but incongruous sewage works, along the grassy bottom of this delightful dry valley.

Ignore paths leading out of the valley, to continue along the valley bottom. When you see a blue arrow on a post, go left here to take a gate by a dew pond. At a three-way fingerpost, go right, around the pond, to follow a wall on your right(this little detour is simply to avoid a small pasture in private ownership).

Walk through an area of gorse bushes, a habitat frequented by linnets and yellowhammers. Soon the landscape is scrubby and stony; as you enter National Trust property you walk through lovely woodland. The valley-sides are highest here, as you approach the limestone crags and screes of Wolfscote Dale ahead, and find yourself on the banks of the River Dove.

*If you want to rest your legs, this is the spot for a sit-down. The sound of the river flowing over a succession of little, man-made ledges is almost soporific, and offers quite a contrast to dry Biggin Dale.*

Go right along the sandy path to enjoy easy walking on the level, with the bubbling River Dove never more than a few metres away. As you leave the

*119*

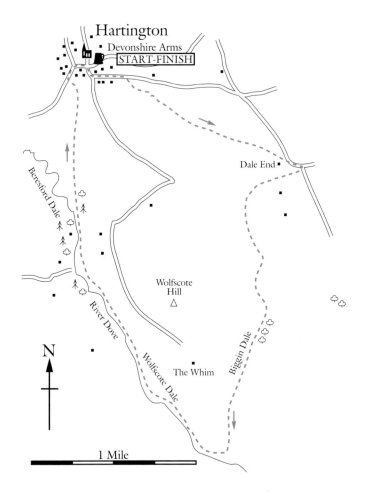

National Trust-owned area of Wolfscote Dale, take a gap-stile to arrive at a meeting of paths and a wooden footbridge spanning the river. Your route is straight ahead, through another gap-stile and across a field. Through a pair of stones carved to create a gap-stile, you cross another footbridge over the Dove.

Go right here, along a good path, now keeping the river to your right. This is well-wooded Beresford Dale: though short it suffers nothing in comparison with Biggin and Wolfscote Dales. Beneath glowing limestone crags your path crosses the river on another footbridge; soon you climb uphill and away from the river.

Through a gate you leave the woodland and emerge into open pasture. You have an unambiguous path across fields and through gap-stiles. Cross a stony track and keep straight ahead, following a Hartington sign. Accompany a wall on your left, to arrive at a road by Rooke's Pottery. Go right and back into the village.

# CRAG INN

*A walk of much variety, from breezy moor tops to the intimate riverside scenery at Three Shires Head*

DISTANCE: 7 miles (12 km)
ALLOW: 3 hours
MAP: OS Outdoor Leisure 24
TERRAIN: Easy
PARKING: Pub walkers can park in the pub's own car-park. Additional roadside parking is available 100m to the north, by the junction with the Buxton Road

The Crag Inn is situated on an unclassified road, 7 miles (12km) south-west of Buxton. Walkers are welcome; the option is either to remove muddy boots or don the plastic overshoes provided. A free house, the pub has a range of real ales and an enticing menu chalked on a blackboard over the open fireplace. Meals are available from 12-2pm (throughout the day in summer). Tel: 01260-227239.

*Wildboarclough is one of the many places in the north of England where the very last wild boar was killed. More recently there were three silk mills here, powered by the water of Clough Brook. Today, bereft of both mills and boars, Wildboarclough is a peaceful little backwater, sheltering beneath a distinctive hill that goes by the fanciful name of Shutlingsloe.*

Walk left out of the Crag Inn, for just 50m, and take a gap-stile in a wall to the right. Cross Clough Brook on a wooden footbridge, continue through conifer woodland and follow a wall

uphill. After a stile at the top of the wood, keep
following the wall. Cross a tiny beck on a wooden
footbridge and walk across the middle of a field, taking
your direction from a waymarker post. Take another
footbridge and head for the top-right corner of the field
to join a walled track uphill. There's a fine view to be had
if you turn around: the pub dwarfed by the symmetrical
contours of Shutlingsloe.

At the top take a step-stile and continue along the field
path, skirting a small conifer plantation. Keep right of a
barn to come to a road; cross via a pair of stiles and walk
up to join a metalled track. After just 100m the track
forks: right is to Heild End Farm, but your route is left,

uphill. The track, now grassy, soon levels out, allowing you to lengthen your stride. You now have easy, breezy walking through an arable landscape; many fields have been 'won' from the open moorland, with stone walls keeping the heather and bracken at bay.

Eventually, the track runs between walls, to a farm and then a road. Notice a house with an elaborate datestone above the door, which features a depiction of an eagle and child. The building was a pub of that name until the First World War.

Cross the road and continue downhill on another farm

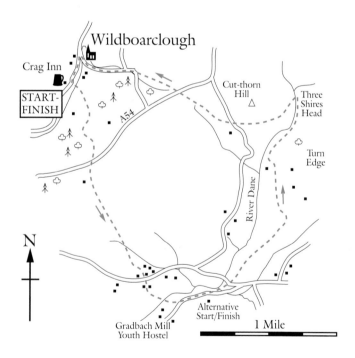

Wildboarclough

Crag Inn

START-FINISH

A54

Cut-thorn Hill

Three Shires Head

Turn Edge

River Dane

N

Alternative Start/Finish

1 Mile

Gradbach Mill
Youth Hostel

track, signed to Gradbach. Walk through a farmyard to join a walled track downhill that passes a barn. About 50m beyond a metal gate take a wooden gate in the wall on the right, to join a path descending to a footbridge across the River Dane, to Gradbach Mill Youth Hostel.

*The austerely symmetrical façade of the building reveals its industrial origins. Built in 1785, to replace an earlier mill that burnt down, Gradbach Mill produced sewing silk with machinery powered by water from the River Dane. When water power ceased to be economic the mill fell into disuse. Though the workers' cottages were demolished, the manager's house and the mill survived.*

Take a metalled track uphill (on the left is the remains of a leat which delivered water to the mill's waterwheel, which no longer survives). Meet a minor road by a pair of stone gateposts; walk left here, downhill, to Gradbach car-park.

(*) 100m beyond the car-park take a footbridge on the left, over a beck (stained orange by iron deposits, often due to flowing through old mine workings). Follow the River Dane to the right, to a road. Bear right here, uphill, for just 100m, to take a waymarked path on the left. Keep to the right of a farmhouse, to another waymarker at a step stile. Cross a field to a gap in the wall, keeping the wall to your left across two more fields. Pass a barn on a stony track that soon reverts to a grassy field-path. Just keep following the wall to your left and you won't go wrong.

When the wall ends abruptly, continue straight ahead across a field, towards a farm on the horizon. Halfway

across the next field, and just 50m before you reach a
ladder-stile over a wall, bear left to join a grassy track.
Cross a stile and follow the track to the right, downhill,
to join a stony farm track. The track goes left, after a
ruined barn, to reach the river once again at a junction of
paths.

Keep right, to follow a waymarker that reads Three
Shires Head, to follow the River Dane upstream. Ignore
a footbridge and keep the river to your left. The waymarked path continues to follow the river (albeit at a
higher level) through a pleasant landscape of bracken,
dry-stone walls and wind-tossed trees. Soon you arrive in
the sheltered environs of Three Shires Head.

*As the name suggests, the borders of three counties –
Derbyshire, Cheshire and Staffordshire – meet at this
delightful spot. A beck meets the infant River Dane in a
series of little waterfalls, and the river is spanned by the
single arch of a stone packhorse bridge. An old reputation
for lawlessness in these parts (including illegal cock-fights
and counterfeiting) stems from the miscreants being able to
cross the border at will, to escape the attentions of any one
county's policemen.*

Cross the bridge and take a good path to the left,
climbing very gradually out of the valley and around the
flank of Cut-thorn Hill. At a road walk right, uphill, for
just 20m, before taking a stile on your left. Walk behind a
house to come out shortly on open moorland. Though
the route is less distinct here, it is still easy to follow –
uphill and over a wall-stile as the familiar shape of
Shutlingsloe reappears beyond the immediate horizon.

You have level walking now, on a cinder track. Cross the A54 road and continue in the same direction (though you may have to walk around a couple of boggy bits). Pass a barn and head for the right-hand corner of a conifer plantation, where you will find a gate. Take a track down to a road and walk right, downhill, keeping left when the road forks. Pass the neat sandstone church of St Saviour's and go left at a T-junction to arrive back at the Crag Inn.

## Other Dalesman titles for walkers

### *Walks Around Series: Yorkshire*
*Grassington* Richard Musgrave £1.99
*Ilkley & Otley* Colin Speakman £2.99
*Nidderdale* Dorian Speakman £2.99
*Settle & Malham* Richard Musgrave £1.99
*Skipton* Mark Reid £2.99
*Swaledale* Sheila Bowker £2.99
*Three Peaks* Colin Speakman £2.99
*Wensleydale* Sheila Bowker £2.99
*Yorkshire Coast* Malcolm Boyes £2.99

### *Walks Around Series: Lake District*
*Ambleside* Tom Bowker £2.99
*Coniston & Hawkshead* Mary Welsh £2.99
*Keswick* Dawn Gibson £2.99
*Ullswater* Mary Welsh £2.99
*Windermere* Robert Gambles £2.99

### *Walks Around Series: Lancashire*
*Clitheroe* Terry Marsh £2.99
*Lancaster* Terry Marsh £2.99

### *Pub Walks Series*
*Lake District* Terry Marsh £5.99
*North York Moors* Richard Musgrave £5.99
*Yorkshire Dales* Richard Musgrave £5.99

### *Long-Distance Walks*
*Cumbria Way* John Trevelyan £2.99

### *Safety for Walkers*
*Map Reading* Robert Matkin £3.99

Available from all good bookshops.
In case of difficulty, or for a full list of Dalesman titles, contact:
Country Publications Ltd
The Water Mill, Broughton Hall, Skipton, North Yorkshire BD23 3AG.
*Tel:* (+44) 01756 701033
*Website:* www.countrypublications.co.uk